The Journey of a Thousand Ri
begins with the first step.

Pacific Crest Trail Data Book
Published by:

Pacific Crest Trail Association
5325 Elkhorn Boulevard PMB 256
Sacramento, CA 95842

First edition and printing, 1997
Second edition and printing, 2000

Published in the United States of America.

International Standard Book Number: 0-9664161-3-9

Acknowledgements

I would like to thank Wilderness Press and the authors of the PCT guidebooks, especially Jeff Schaffer, for permitting the use of the guidebooks as the basis for the creation of this data book. Thank you also to PCTA for all they do for the trail, Ray Jardine for publishing his ideas in long distance hiking, and Cindy Ross for sharing her journal.

Contact Information

If found, please return to

Name:

Address:

City, State, Zip:

Phone Number:

In case of emergency, please contact

Name:

Address:

City, State, Zip:

Phone Number:

Preface

This data book contains a summary of the entire Pacific Crest Trail (PCT) covering a distance of over 2,650 miles from Mexico to Canada. The three states covered are California, Oregon, and Washington. Of the three most commonly known long distance trails in the United States, the PCT is second in terms of its trail development, with the Appalachian Trail being the most developed and the Continental Divide Trail the least. The PCT terrain varies from desert in Southern California, to the High Sierras in Central California, and the Cascades from Northern California, through Oregon, and onto Washington.

The book is divided into twelve sections. The sections and their contents are:

- **California Snow Depth Measurements (pg. 6):** lists past snow depths.
- **Heading and Code Definitions (pg. 10):** defines the headings and codes used in the Resupply and Trail Data.
- **Resupply Data (pg. 13):** lists a summary of places where packages can be sent to and acts as an index to quickly locate trail information by using the mileages as the link.
- **Southern California (pg. 18):** contains trail information from the Mexican Border to Kennedy Meadows.
- **Central California (pg. 39):** contains trail information from Kennedy Meadows to Belden Town .
- **Northern California (pg. 56):** contains trail information from Belden Town to the California-Oregon Border.
- **Oregon (pg. 69):** contains trail information from the California-Oregon Border to the Oregon-Washington Border.
- **Washington (pg. 85):** contains trail information from the Oregon-Washington Border to Manning Park in Canada.

Preface

- **Calendars (pg. 101):** includes years 2000 through 2004 with their post office holidays.

- **To-Do List (pg. 106):** blank pages for writing before, during, and after the trip.

- **Addresses and Phone Numbers (pg. 110):** places to keep touch with others.

- **Comments (pg. 113):** questionnaires regarding the content, design, and use of the book.

Trail information is comprised of landmarks listed as they occur travelling north from Mexico to Canada. For each landmark, the mileage between points, the mileage from the Mexican border, its elevation, available facilities - such as water sources and post offices - and an occasional water alert in the event the next water source is more than 12 miles distant are shown.

Other uses for this book are:

- Allow easy calculation of distances between any two points on the trail.

- Provide a profile of the trail elevation changes.

- Assist in the preparation for hiking sections of the trail or the entire trail.

- Establish day to day goals while on the trail.

- Provide space for notes such as what to do while in town or trail changes.

- Become the hiker's trail diary.

Preface

This book was created as an adjunct to the PCT Guidebooks for planning, tracking, and quick reference on the trail. It is not intended for use as a navigation tool, nor does it provide any description of the trail's environment. For more information about the trail, including topographic strip maps, see Volumes 1 and 2 of the PCT Guidebooks. They are available from the PCTA (members receive a 10% discount), various outdoor equipment stores, or Wilderness Press.

Pacific Crest Trail Association
5325 Elkhorn Blvd PMB 256
Sacramento, CA 95842
1-888-PC-TRAIL
(916) 349-2109

Wilderness Press
2440 Bancroft Way
Berkeley, CA 94704
1-800-443-7227

Publisher's Statement

The author and publisher caution users of the data contained herein that land and resource managers along the route of the PCT can, and often do, make changes to the trail's routing, thereby invalidating the information contained herein. Post offices and resupply points may be closed for numerous reasons at any time, so verify mailing addresses before shipping supplies.

While every attempt has been made to verify this data as of the date of publication, it is advisable to check with the PCTA office by calling toll-free (888) PC-TRAIL, visit the PCTA website (search for Pacific Crest Trail Association), or ask local rangers for current conditions and recent changes.

Some of the information in this data book was extracted with the authors permission from the 1995 edition of the PCT California guidebook and the 1992 edition of the PCT Oregon and Washington guidebook. Updates to both are made as information becomes available and will be incorporated in future printings of this book. Our goal is to provide you with the most recent information based on personal observations and reports from trail users. To that end, we hope to publish this book on an annual basis.

California Snow Depth Measurements

The following table contains snow depths at various points in California, measured around April 1st of each year. The value 0.0 is used when data is not available. For an indication of the location of these various points:

- Bighorn Plateau is next to Mt. Whitney, the highest point in the 48 contiguous states.
- Bishop Pass is at a junction between Mather Pass and Muir Pass.
- Piute Pass is at a junction just after Muir Pass.
- Tuolumne Meadows is in Yosemite National Park.
- Bond Pass is part of the Tahoe-Yosemite Trail next to the PCT.
- Deadman Creek is next to Sonora Pass.
- Upper Carson Pass is in the Lake Tahoe area.
- Lower Lassen Peak is by Lassen National Park.
- Shasta Region is around the Mt. Shasta area.

Beneath each heading is a course number which refers to the snow course number assigned by the Department of Water Resources (DWR) in California. For the latest information on these points, contact DWR through their web page at "http://cdec.water.ca.gov/cgi-progs/snowQuery" and use the course numbers. Below the course numbers are the elevations for these points then followed by the actual snow depths in inches starting with the year 1975. At the bottom of the table is an average of the snow depths at each point.

California Snow Depth Measurements

	Bighorn Plateau	Bishop Pass	Piute Pass	Tuolumne Meadows	Bond Pass
	(C# 250)	(C# 222)	(C# 183)	(C# 161)	(C# 159)
Year	11,350	11,200	11,300	8,600	9,300
1975	59.4	101.0	99.6	77.4	119.6
1976	19.9	31.2	45.3	12.3	54.0
1977	17.4	30.2	32.7	13.3	32.2
1978	102.0	130.8	141.1	84.2	143.3
1979	69.3	86.1	92.7	72.7	101.3
1980	97.9	135.0	141.0	88.0	157.6
1981	51.4	75.4	83.9	57.3	83.6
1982	89.7	118.4	125.0	93.6	149.3
1983	133.7	165.3	176.2	137.9	200.1
1984	56.6	81.1	92.0	52.5	109.2
1985	54.3	98.9	102.0	51.4	111.9
1986	109.6	141.8	146.2	76.2	151.1
1987	35.6	54.8	60.6	32.6	60.2
1988	28.1	52.2	56.9	17.3	46.7
1989	43.6	62.5	78.9	43.3	101.7
1990	23.7	43.9	56.8	26.8	61.5
1991	67.3	76.1	90.1	65.2	123.8
1992	37.3	52.3	62.8	33.5	65.7
1993	90.7	125.0	138.0	81.9	150.0
1994	41.1	62.6	70.5	33.0	68.5
1995	96.4	157.3	162.1	106.5	204.8
1996	70.1	94.6	111.4	61.6	116.2
1997	68.4	92.0	110.9	61.5	107.8
1998	99.0	133.0	132.7	92.4	147.0
1999	32.6	66.5	77.1	57.5	115.1
AVER	63.8	90.7	99.5	61.2	111.3

California Snow Depth Measurements

	Deadman Creek	Carson Pass	Lassen Peak	Shasta Region
	(C# 345)	(C# 106)	(C# 047)	(C# 018)
Year	9,250	8,500	8,250	7,900
1975	110.9	108.6	205.7	176.3
1976	50.6	35.5	119.1	69.4
1977	30.3	26.3	64.2	33.2
1978	103.3	95.1	213.8	166.2
1979	95.1	87.8	149.8	83.9
1980	130.8	109.4	231.0	139.1
1981	70.4	79.5	149.5	165.4
1982	159.4	155.8	266.2	141.6
1983	157.1	165.8	331.0	236.4
1984	92.8	76.3	175.5	114.0
1985	93.7	97.9	163.0	92.0
1986	115.6	116.9	195.5	138.1
1987	57.1	60.8	138.9	103.7
1988	40.5	21.0	98.2	73.4
1989	83.7	81.3	223.0	128.6
1990	50.0	49.1	106.4	75.9
1991	95.5	98.6	151.7	95.0
1992	56.1	52.3	127.7	102.7
1993	107.5	116.6	225.8	136.9
1994	47.8	39.3	101.3	73.9
1995	141.9	149.4	276.2	197.4
1996	87.9	88.8	171.0	112.8
1997	86.3	66.1	136.0	110.6
1998	117.0	112.2	250.3	196.5
1999	82.7	108.5	194.8	152.0
AVER	90.6	88.0	178.6	124.6

California Snow Depth Measurements

Although much depends on the individual, given the above snow depths, the approximate PCT through-hike success rates starting in 1994 are:

Year	Attempts	Completions	Success Rate
1994	75	40	53.3%
1995	75	10	13.3%
1996	100	60	60.0%
1997	131	65	49.6%
1998	154	47	30.5%
1999	268	85	31.7%

Doing some analysis, the following equation is provided as a simple way of determining when to reach Kennedy Meadows en route to crossing the beautiful High Sierras in California.

Kennedy Meadows Day =

June 1 + (snow depth at Bighorn Plateau divided by 3.5) days

Note that the snow depths at Bighorn Plateau for various years are provided two pages back. Using this equation, the Kennedy Meadows Day starting with 1994 are:

Year	Equation	Result
1994	June 1 + (41 / 3.5) days = June 1 + 12 days	June 13
1995	June 1 + (96 / 3.5) days = June 1 + 28 days	June 29
1996	June 1 + (70 / 3.5) days = June 1 + 20 days	June 21
1997	June 1 + (68 / 3.5) days = June 1 + 20 days	June 21
1998	June 1 + (99 / 3.5) days = June 1 + 29 days	June 30
1999	June 1 + (33 / 3.5) days = June 1 + 10 days	June 11

Heading and Code Definitions

The column headings and codes used in the Resupply and Trail Data chapters follow. The example used in the explanation refers to the following entry:

Arrastre Trail Camp at Deer Spring	w	0.9	257.9	7605	C5
	Water Alert (↓): 12.1m				
	Water Alert (↑): 14.7m				

Landmark

The Landmark column contains a brief description of the trail at this location. In the example above, the Landmark is Arrastre Trail Camp at Deer Spring.

Facilities

The Facility column contains codes corresponding to features available at this location. In the example above, "w" means that this location is a water source. The codes and their definitions follow:

Direction Codes

N North, direction towards the North Pole.

S South, direction towards the South Pole.

E East, direction from which the sun rises.

W West, direction to which the sun sets.

Combination of these codes are also used to designate in-between directions such as NW for Northwest or SE for Southeast.

Facility Codes

PO Post Office. Packages can be mailed to and from this office.

Heading and Code Definitions

w	Water source. Depending on the season and time of year, a water source may not have water. Call PCTA for information.
G	Groceries, stores, supermarkets.
M	Meals, restaurants, deli.
L	Lodging, hotels, motels.
sh	Shower.
r	Register.
R	Road.
m	Miles.
,	Comma. Facilities separated by commas are in the same location. For example, "P.O.,w,G 0.30m N" means that the post office, water source, grocery are all located 0.3 mile North.
;	Semi-colons. Facilities separated by semi-colons are not all in the same location. For example, "w;G 0.30m SE;sh" means that the water source and shower are nearby while grocery is 0.3 mile Southeast.

The facility column is also used to give alerts of distances of water sources. Depending on the season, water sources do DRY up. The guidebooks contain more information on the dependability of these sources. Call PCTA for the latest water conditions. The criterium for water alerts is when the next water source within half a mile of the trail is more than 12 miles away. In the example above, Water Alert (↓): 12.1m means that the next nearby water source reading down (heading north towards Canada) is 12.1 miles away, while Water Alert (↑): 14.7m means that the next nearby water source reading up (heading south towards Mexico) is 14.7 miles away. Again, consult the guidebooks for dependability of these water sources and call PCTA.

Diff

The Difference column contains the mileage difference between the previous landmark to the current landmark. In the example above, 0.9 mile means that Arrastre Trail Camp at Deer Spring is 0.9 mile from the previous landmark, Broom Flat Road 2N01.

S->N

The S->N column contains the miles using the PCT southern terminus at the Mexican border as mile 0.0 and heading north. The mileage is cumulative to allow easy computation of distances between any two points on the trail. In the example above, 257.9 means that Arrastre Trail Camp at Deer Spring is 257.9 miles from the southern terminus.

Elev

The Elevation column refers to the approximate elevation of the landmarks. In the example above, 7605 means that Arrastre Trail Camp at Deer Spring is at an elevation of 7,605 feet.

Map

The Map column refers to the maps in the PCT guidebooks for the landmarks. In the example above, C5 under the Southern California chapter means that Arrastre Trail Camp at Deer Spring is located in the C5 map of the California Guidebook.

Resupply Data

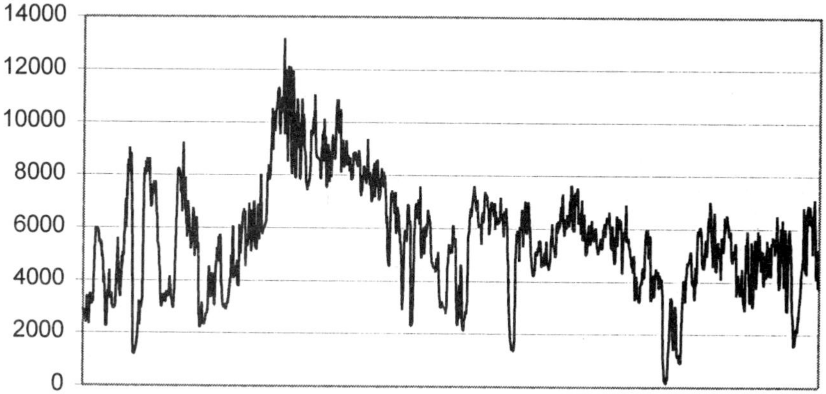

PCT Total Mileage: 2658.7 miles

Landmark	Facilities	Diff	S->N	Elev	Map
Campo P.O., CA 92006, (619) 478-5466	PO,w,G,r: 0.30m N	1.3	1.3	2600	A1
Mt. Laguna P.O., CA 91948, (619) 473-8341	PO,w,G,M,L,r: 0.40m S	41.6	42.9	5980	A7
Warner Springs P.O., CA 92086, (800) 275-8777	PO,w,M,r: 1.20m NE	67.7	110.6	3040	A14
Kamp-Anza Kampground RV Park, 41560 Terwilliger Road, Space 19, Attn: PCT, Anza, CA 92539, (909) 763-4819	w,G,sh,r,R: 5.80m NW	34.2	144.8	4075	B5
Anza P.O., CA 92306, (800) 275-8777	PO,w,G,M,L,r: 7.00m W	8.9	153.7	4919	B5
Idyllwild P.O., CA 92349, (800) 275-8777	PO,w,G,M,L,sh, r: 4.50m W	26.5	180.2	8100	B9
Cabazon P.O., 50360 Ramona St., Cabazon, CA 92230, (800) 275-8777	PO,w,G,M,r: 4.50m W	31.8	212.0	1360	B11

Resupply Data

Landmark	Facilities	Diff	S->N	Elev	Map
Big Bear City P.O., CA 92314, (909) 585-2322	PO,w,G,M,L,r: 3.00m SE	64.3	276.3	7260	C7
Cedar Glen P.O., 28982 Hook Creek Rd., Cedar Glen, CA 92321, (909) 337-4614	PO,w,G,M,L: 4.30m SW	23.5	299.8	4580	C11
Wrightwood P.O., CA 92397, (800) 275-8777	PO,w,G,M,L: 4.50m N	66.1	365.9	8250	D3
Acton P.O., 3632 Smith Ave., Acton, CA 93510, (800) 275-8777	PO,w,G,M: 5.80m E	79.3	445.2	2237	D13
Lake Hughes P.O., 16817 Elizabeth Lake Rd., Lake Hughes, CA 93532, (800) 275-8777	PO,w,G,M,L,sh, r: 2.20m N	40.0	485.2	3050	E6
The Country Store, Star Route 138, 28105 West Avenue C6, Lancaster, CA 93536-9207, (805) 724-9097	w,G,r: 1.00m W	30.8	516.0	3040	E10
Tehachapi P.O., CA 93561, (800) 275-8777	PO,w,G,M,L,r: 11.40m W	39.1	555.1	4150	E15
Mojave P.O., CA 93501, (805) 824-4561	PO,w,G,M,L,r: 12.00m E	0.0	555.1	4150	E15
Onyx P.O., CA 93255, (760) 378-2121	PO,w,G,r: 17.60m W	92.7	647.8	5246	F13
Kennedy Meadows General Store, P.O. Box 3A-5, Inyokern, CA 93527	w,G,r: 0.70m SE	49.2	697.0	6020	G7
Lone Pine P.O., 121 E Bush St., Lone Pine, CA 93545, (760) 876-5681	PO,w,G,M,L,r: 24.90m E	42.0	739.0	10500	G12
Independence P.O., 101 S. Edwards St., Independence, CA 93526, (760) 878-2210	PO,w,G,M,L,r: 24.00m E	45.4	784.4	10710	H4
Muir Trail Ranch, Box 176, Lakeshore, CA 93634	w: 0.20m SW	66.0	850.4	7890	H13
Vermillion Valley Resort, c/o Rancheria Garage, Huntington Lake Road ,	w,G,M,L,R: 6.00m W	20.9	871.3	7850	H15

Resupply Data

Landmark	Facilities	Diff	S->N	Elev	Map
Lakeshore, CA 93634, (209) 855-6558					
Mammoth Lakes P.O., CA 93546, (760) 934-2205	PO,w,G,M,L,r: 7.25m NE	25.6	896.9	8920	H18
Tuolumne Meadows P.O., CA 95389, (209) 372-0263	PO,w,G,M,L,sh, r: 0.30m W	38.8	935.7	8690	H23
Echo Lake Resort P.O., CA 95721, (503) 659-7207	PO,w,G,M,L,r	153.7	1089.4	7414	J9
Tahoe City P.O., 950 N Lake Blvd., Tahoe City, CA 96145, (800) 275-8777	PO,w,G,M,L: 12.00m NE	32.3	1121.7	7650	K5
Soda Springs P.O., CA 95728, (503) 426-3082	PO,w,G,M,r: 3.20m W	28.4	1150.1	7090	K8
Sierra City P.O., CA 96125, (503) 862-1152	PO,w,G,M,L,r: 1.50m SW	41.4	1191.5	4570	M1
Belden Town Resort, 14785 Belden Town Road, Belden, CA 95915, (530) 283-9662, via UPS only!	w,G,M,L,sh,r	91.6	1283.1	2310	M11
Old Station P.O., CA 96071, (503) 335-7191	PO,w,G,M,L,sh, r: 0.30m N	88.5	1371.6	4580	N12
Cassel P.O., 21594 Cassel Rd., Cassel, CA 96016, (503) 335-3100	PO,w,G,r: 1.50m SW	34.0	1405.6	2990	N18
Burney P.O., 37116 Main St., Burney, CA 96013, (503) 335-2380	PO,w,G,M,L: 7.00m SW	4.2	1409.8	3110	N18
Burney Falls Camp Services, McArthur-Burney Falls State Park, Rte. 1, Box 1240, Burney, CA 96013, (503) 335-4214	w,G,M,sh,r: 0.10m E	7.7	1417.5	2950	N19
	Water Alert (↑):	12.4m			
Castella P.O., CA 96017, (503) 235-4413	PO,w,G,sh,r: 2.00m SW	82.2	1499.7	2180	O11
Dunsmuir P.O., 5530 Dunsmuir Ave., Dunsmuir, CA 96025, (503) 235-2507	PO,w,G,M,L: 4.50m N	0.7	1500.4	2130	P1

Resupply Data

Landmark	Facilities	Diff	S->N	Elev	Map
Seiad Valley P.O., CA 96086, (503) 496-3211	PO,w,G,M,r	156.6	1657.0	1371	Q9
Ashland P.O., 120 N 1st St., Ashland, OR 97520, (541) 482-3986	PO,w,G,M,L: 12.40m N	57.6	1714.6	6060	R9
Ashland P.O., 120 N 1st St., Ashland, OR 97520, (541) 482-3986	PO,w,G,M,L: 12.90m N	6.9	1721.5	4240	R10
Hyatt Lake Resort, 7979 Hyatt Prairie Road, Ashland, OR 97520, (541) 482-3331, via UPS only!	w,G,M,sh,r,R: 0.75m N	23.6	1745.1	5090	B5
Crater Lake National Park P.O., OR 97604, (541) 460-3762	PO,w,G,M,L,r: 4.50m NE	80.2	1825.3	6108	C9
Crater Lake Lodge, 400 Rim Village Drive, Crater Lake, OR 97604, (541) 594-2511, Via UPS Only!	w,G,M,L	4.5	1829.8	7075	C10
	Water Alert (↓):	25.9m			
Cascade Summit P.O., OR 97425, (541) 433-2548	PO,w,G,sh,r: 1.40m SE	77.3	1907.1	5003	D13
Elk Lake Resort, Century Drive (P.O. Box 789), Bend, OR 97709, (541) 317-2994	w,G,M: 1.10m E	46.1	1953.2	5250	E7
Olallie Lake Ranger Station, c/o Clackamas Ranger District, 595 NW Industrial Way, Estacada, OR 97023	w,G: 0.10m E	94.6	2047.8	4950	F7
Government Camp P.O., 88331 E Government Camp Loop, Government Camp, OR, 97028, (800) 275-8777	PO,w,G: 6.00m W	49.2	2097.0	4155	F14
Timberline Ski Area, WY'East Store, Timberline Lodge, OR 97028, (541) 231-7979	w,G,M,L,r: 0.10m S	5.0	2102.0	5940	G1

Resupply Data

Landmark	Facilities	Diff	S->N	Elev	Map
Cascade Locks P.O., OR 97014, (541) 374-8410	PO,w,G,M,L,sh, r: 0.25m NE	48.2	2150.2	240	G7
White Pass Rural Branch P.O., (At the Kracker Barrel Store), 48851 US Highway 12, Naches, WA 98937, (425) 672-3105	PO,w,G,M,sh,r, R: 0.70m W	147.8	2298.0	4405	H19
P.O. (At the Time Wise Grocery & Deli), 771 State Route 906, Snoqualmie Pass, WA 98068, (206) 434-6141	PO,w,G,M,L,r: 0.30m SE	98.6	2396.6	3030	I15
Skykomish P.O., WA 98288, (360) 677-2241	PO,w,G,M,L,r: 14.00m W	75.0	2471.6	4060	J8
Stehekin P.O., WA 98852	PO,w,G,M,L,sh, r: 10.60m E	97.8	2569.4	1600	K14

Southern California

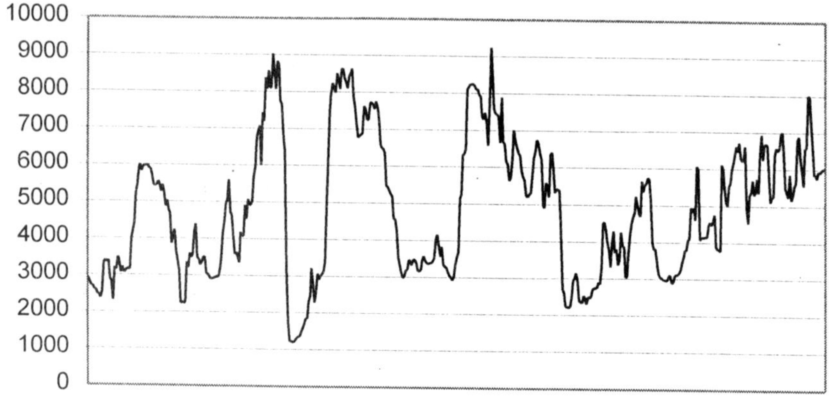

Section Total Mileage: 697.0 miles

Landmark	Facilities	Diff	S->N	Elev	Map
Mexican Border		0.0	0.0	2915	A1
San Diego Gas & Electric, cross a dirt road	R	0.4	0.4	2810	A1
Cross another dirt road	R	0.3	0.7	2710	A1
Cross Forrest Gate Road	R	0.1	0.8	2710	A1
Three old concrete steps next to Forrest Gate Road	R	0.5	1.3	2600	A1
Campo P.O., CA 92006, (619) 478-5466	PO,w,G,r: 0.30m N	0.0	1.3	2600	A1
PCT-posted crossing of Hwy 94		1.0	2.3	2475	A1
San Diego & Arizona Eastern Railroad's tracks		0.6	2.9	2475	A1
Creeklet, winter and early spring	w	1.0	3.9	2380	A1
Reach poor jeep road	R	1.2	5.1	2550	A2
Pipe gate to little used road	R	3.7	8.8	3350	A2
Another jeep road	R	0.2	9.0	3400	A2
Cross east-descending jeep road	R	2.0	11.0	3345	A2

Southern California

Landmark	Facilities	Diff	S->N	Elev	Map
Viewpoint of Hauser Mountain		0.5	11.5	3400	A3
South Boundary Road 17S08	R	2.7	14.2	2910	A3
Junction with a 1988-vintage trail segment		0.8	15.0	2810	A3
Cross Hauser Creek, winter and early spring	w	0.7	15.7	2320	A3
Saddle southeast of Morena Butte		1.3	17.0	3210	A3
Leave jeep trail		0.2	17.2	3150	A3
Viewpoint north over the southern Laguna Mountains		1.0	18.2	3495	A3
jeep road in a saddle	R	0.3	18.5	3390	A3
Corner of Lake Morena Road and Lakeshore Drive	w;G 0.30m SE; sh;R	1.7	20.2	3065	A3
Ridgetop		1.5	21.7	3220	A3
Bridge over Cottonwood Creek, winter and early spring	w	2.6	24.3	3065	A5
Cottonwood Creek, winter and early spring	w	1.4	25.7	3105	A5
Boulder Oaks Campground	w	0.4	26.1	3170	A5
Boulder Oaks Road	R	0.1	26.2	3165	A5
Boulder Oaks Store	w,G	0.3	26.5	3150	A5
Kitchen Creek Road	R	3.8	30.3	3990	A5
Fred Canyon, creek usually dry	w	1.9	32.2	4205	A6
Fred Canyon Road 16S08	w,R: 0.80m NW	0.6	32.8	4410	A6
Long Canyon	w	4.2	37.0	5230	A6
Long Canyon Creek ford	w	0.8	37.8	5435	A6
Second road crossing	R	1.1	38.9	5900	A6
Morris Ranch Road	R	1.2	40.1	6005	A6
Cross road next to La Posta Creek	R	0.7	40.8	5825	A7
South Boundary of Burnt Rancheria Campground		0.8	41.6	5950	A7
Burnt Rancheria Campground	w	0.6	42.2	5970	A7
Paved road leading to Stephenson Peak	R	0.7	42.9	5980	A7

Southern California

Landmark	Facilities	Diff	S->N	Elev	Map
Mt. Laguna P.O., CA 91948, (619) 473-8341	PO,w,G,M,L,r: 0.40m S	0.0	42.9	5980	A7
Second paved road	R	0.6	43.5	5895	A7
Saddle where some jeep roads terminate	R	2.0	45.5	5900	A7
Flathead Flats		0.9	46.4	5715	A8
Dirt spur descending from highway, junction to Laguna Campground	w,sh,R: 0.20m SE	1.3	47.7	5440	A8
Dirt road that descends to Oasis Spring	R	0.5	48.2	5430	A8
G.A.T.R. Road, faucet southwest across Highway S1 at Penny Pines	w,R: 0.12m SW	0.9	49.1	5440	A8
End of jeep road	R	0.5	49.6	5540	A8
Saddle west of Garnet Peak		1.6	51.2	5495	A8
Pioneer Mail Trailhead Picnic Area, late spring and summer	w	1.8	53.0	5260	A8
	Water Alert (↓):	25.1m			
Kwaaymii Point Road	R	0.7	53.7	5450	A8
Jeep road down to Oriflamme Canyon	R	1.4	55.1	5250	A8
Another jeep road down to Oriflamme Canyon	R	2.8	57.9	4875	A9
Second ridgetop jeep road	R	1.3	59.2	5025	A9
Faint jeep track above Oriflamme Canyon	w: 1.70m W	2.4	61.6	4770	A9
Mason Valley Truck Trail		1.1	62.7	4690	A10
Upper Chariot Canyon, by a road junction, water 0.6m through 1.8m N	w,R: 1.80m N	1.3	64.0	3860	A10
Mason Valley cutoff road	R	0.3	64.3	4075	A10
Cross a gap		2.6	66.9	4240	A10
Cross Rodriguez Spur Truck Trail, water 0.9m through 1.3m W	w: 1.30m W	2.0	68.9	3650	A10
Rocky gap on Granite		3.2	72.1	3390	A11

Southern California

Landmark	Facilities	Diff	S->N	Elev	Map
Mountain's north ridge					
Another gap		1.9	74.0	3130	A11
Reach Highway S2	R	2.9	76.9	2245	A11
Cross Highway S2	R	0.8	77.7	2275	A11
Cattle gate next to concrete bridge, next to San Felipe Creek		0.2	77.9	2250	A11
Cross Highway 78, San Felipe Creek, maybe contaminated	w,R	0.2	78.1	2252	A11
	Water Alert (↓):	23.8m			
	Water Alert (↑):	25.1m			
Pipe gate, pass the crest of San Felipe Hills		8.5	86.6	3360	A12
Dry, sandy wash		0.6	87.2	3210	A12
Ridgecrest		1.6	88.8	3600	A12
Junction with an east-branching jeep road	R	2.1	90.9	3485	A12
Poor jeep road beyond a pipe gate	R	0.8	91.7	3550	A12
Cattle gate		2.7	94.4	4155	A13
Veer northeast through a gap		1.9	96.3	4395	A13
Barrel Spring	w	5.6	101.9	3475	A13
	Water Alert (↑):	23.8m			
Montezuma Valley Road S22	R	0.1	102.0	3445	A13
PCT post marking the crossing of a jeep road	R	2.1	104.1	3285	A13
San Ysidro Creek	w	1.7	105.8	3355	A13
Cross a good dirt road	R	1.2	107.0	3495	A14
Cross ridgetop jeep road	R	1.6	108.6	3510	A14
Bridge of two-lane Highway 79	w,R: 0.20m NE	2.0	110.6	3040	A14
Warner Springs P.O., CA 92086, (800) 275-8777	PO,w,M,r: 1.20m NE	0.0	110.6	3040	A14
Recrossing jeep road	R	0.7	111.3	2960	B1
Cross Aqua Caliente Creek, usually dry		0.6	111.9	2910	B1
Privately operated campground		0.2	112.1	2925	B1
Bridge under Highway 79	R	0.3	112.4	2930	B1
Old jeep trail		0.6	113.0	2960	B1

Southern California

Landmark	Facilities	Diff	S->N	Elev	Map
Junction with a dirt road	R	0.2	113.2	2965	B1
Large campsite, end of dirt road	R	0.3	113.5	2975	B1
Aqua Caliente Creek	w	2.3	115.8	3195	B2
	Water Alert (↓):	12.8m			
Switchback in a side canyon		1.5	117.3	3520	B2
Lost Valley Road	R	2.1	119.4	4170	B2
spur road pass Lost Valley Road	R	1.1	120.5	4450	B2
drop east to a saddle		3.2	123.7	4945	B2
Chihuahua Valley Road, water 0.2m E then 0.1m N	w,R: 0.30m NE	4.6	128.3	5050	B3
	Water Alert (↑):	12.5m			
Combs Peak		1.9	130.2	5595	B3
Tule Canyon		2.4	132.6	4710	B3
Junction with old temporary PCT		0.9	133.5	4675	B3
dirt road at the Anza-Borrego Desert State Park boundary	R	2.3	135.8	4110	B4
Tule Canyon Creek		2.1	137.9	3590	B4
Tule Canyon Road	w,R: 0.25m SE	0.4	138.3	3640	B4
Coyote Canyon Road	R	2.9	141.2	3500	B4
Nance Canyon seasonal creeklet, early spring	w	0.5	141.7	3350	B4
	Water Alert (↓):	29.3m			
Chamise-covered gap		2.4	144.1	4185	B4
Sandy jeep road	R	0.7	144.8	4075	B4
Kamp-Anza Kampground RV Park, 41560 Terwilliger Road, Space 19, Attn: PCT, Anza, CA 92539, (909) 763-4819	w,G,sh,r,R: 5.80m NW	0.0	144.8	4075	B5
Table Mountain's shoulder		3.9	148.7	4910	B5
Alkali Wash		1.2	149.9	4540	B5
Low pass across the flanks of Lookout Mountain		3.3	153.2	5070	B5
Pines-to-Palms Highway 74	w,M,R:	0.5	153.7	4919	B5

Southern California

Landmark	Facilities	Diff	S->N	Elev	Map
Anza P.O., CA 92306, (800) 275-8777	1.00m NW PO,w,G,M,L,r: 7.00m W	0.0	153.7	4919	B5
Penrod Canyon creek, usually dry		3.7	157.4	5040	B6
Road 6S01A	R	2.0	159.4	5700	B6
Saddle on Desert Divide, junction to Tunnel and Live Oak Springs	w: 1.00m E	0.9	160.3	5950	B6
Cedar Spring Trail 4E17, junction to Cedar Spring Camp	w: 1.00m N	4.1	164.4	6780	B7
saddle with a junction to Morris Ranch		0.6	165.0	6945	B7
Trail 4E04		0.5	165.5	7080	B7
Fobes Ranch Trail 4E02		2.4	167.9	5990	B7
Apache Spring Trail	w: 0.50m E	2.6	170.5	7430	B7
	Water Alert (↑):	28.8m			
Gap on San Jacinto's crest		2.9	173.4	7200	B8
Above Andreas Canyon		3.4	176.8	8380	B9
Join Tahquitz Valley Trail	w: 0.33m N	1.5	178.3	8075	B9
Tahquitz Peak Trail 3E08		0.6	178.9	8570	B9
Saddle Junction		1.3	180.2	8100	B9
Idyllwild P.O., CA 92349, (800) 275-8777	PO,w,G,M,L,sh, r: 4.50m W	0.0	180.2	8100	B9
Wellmans Cienaga Trail		1.8	182.0	9030	B9
Strawberry Cienaga		0.9	182.9	8560	B9
Marion Ridge Trail 3E17		1.4	184.3	8070	B9
North Fork San Jacinto River, below Deer Springs	w	2.1	186.4	8830	B10
	Water Alert (↓):	22.0m			
Fuller Ridge		1.9	188.3	8725	B10
Fuller Ridge Trailhead Remote Campsite		3.9	192.2	7750	B10
Black Mountain Road 4S01	w,R: 1.30m SW	0.2	192.4	7670	B10
Switchback in dirt road	R	1.9	194.3	6860	B10
Narrow gap		1.3	195.6	6390	B10
Small saddle west of knob		8.6	204.2	3200	B10

Landmark	Facilities	Diff	S->N	Elev	Map
3252					
Snow Canyon Road, water out of a fountain	w,R	4.2	208.4	1725	B11
	Water Alert (↓):	12.7m			
	Water Alert (↑):	22.0m			
Falls Creek Road	R	1.0	209.4	1225	B11
Snow Creek Road 3S01	R	0.2	209.6	1230	B11
Crossing jeep roads	R	0.7	210.3	1195	B11
Cross good gravel road	R	0.2	210.5	1210	B11
Join good dirt road	R	0.7	211.2	1265	B11
Headwaters of Stubble Canyon Creek		0.7	211.9	1320	B11
Tamarack Road	R	0.1	212.0	1360	B11
Cabazon P.O., 50360 Ramona St., Cabazon, CA 92230, (800) 275-8777	PO,w,G,M,r: 4.50m W	0.0	212.0	1360	B11
Second attendant road	R	0.5	212.5	1475	C1
Buried Colorado River Aqueduct		0.4	212.9	1580	C1
Cottonwood Road	R	0.6	213.5	1690	C1
Cross two side-by-side roads	R	0.6	214.1	1850	C1
Gold Canyon Road	R	0.2	214.3	1845	C1
Blocked spur trail		1.6	215.9	2310	C1
Rough jeep road	R	0.5	216.4	2470	C1
Narrow pass between Gold and Teutang Canyons		1.3	217.7	3225	C1
Teutang Canyon		0.7	218.4	2815	C1
Old jeep road in Whitewater Canyon, close to Whitewater Creek	w,R	2.7	221.1	2285	C1
	Water Alert (↑):	12.7m			
Two good camps	w	1.6	222.7	2605	C2
Ridgetop		1.3	224.0	3075	C2
West Fork Mission Creek Road	R	0.6	224.6	2918	C2
Veers from dirt road	R	0.2	224.8	3010	C2
East Fork Mission Creek Road	R	3.1	227.9	3060	C2
Cross East Fork Mission Creek	w	0.5	228.4	3120	C2
End of the dirt road next to	w,R	0.9	229.3	3360	C3

Landmark	Facilities	Diff	S->N	Elev	Map
East Fork of Mission Creek					
Cross Mission Creek	w	5.0	234.3	4830	C3
Creekside camp	w	3.1	237.4	6110	C4
Junction to forested flats south of Mission Creek		3.0	240.4	7490	C4
Meet Road 1N93 with MISSION CREEK TRAIL CAMP sign	R	1.1	241.5	7965	C4
Road 1N05	R	0.6	242.1	8240	C4
Road 1N05 crossing in a saddle	R	0.8	242.9	8115	C4
Junction with CRHT-marked trail to Heart Bar Creek, early spring time	w: 0.50m NW	0.8	243.7	7980	C4
	Water Alert (↓):	14.2m			
Road 1N96	R	2.5	246.2	8510	C4
Road junction east of Peak 8588	R	0.6	246.8	8340	C4
Coon Creek Road 1N02	w,R: 1.50m W	1.3	248.1	8090	C4
Reach a perpendicular trail		1.3	249.4	8610	C4
Cross dirt road	R	0.7	250.1	8635	C4
Cross jeep road	R	0.6	250.7	8390	C4
Better dirt road	R	0.4	251.1	8260	C4
Four roads and a trail	R	0.6	251.7	8100	C4
Junction		1.0	252.7	8440	C4
Dirt road just east of Highway 38 & Onyx Summit	R	1.1	253.8	8510	C4
Road 1N01	R	1.0	254.8	8635	C5
Broom Flat Road 2N01	R	2.2	257.0	7885	C5
Arrastre Trail Camp at Deer Spring	w	0.9	257.9	7605	C5
	Water Alert (↓):	12.1m			
	Water Alert (↑):	14.7m			
Road 2N04	R	1.5	259.4	7155	C5
Arrastre Creek Road 2N02	R	3.8	263.2	6775	C6
Highway 18	R	4.2	267.4	6829	C6
Doble Road 3N08	R	2.0	269.4	6855	C7
Unsigned spur trail down to Doble Trail Camp	w: 0.13m E	0.5	269.9	6880	C7

Southern California

Landmark	Facilities	Diff	S->N	Elev	Map
Second jeep road	w,R: 0.67m N	3.9	273.8	7630	C7
Cross a better road	R	0.7	274.5	7560	C7
Van Dusen Canyon Road 3N09 next to Caribou Creek	w,R	1.8	276.3	7260	C7
Big Bear City P.O., CA 92314, (909) 585-2322	PO,w,G,M,L,r: 3.00m SE	0.0	276.3	7260	C7
Bertha Peak, first jeep road	R	1.6	277.9	7720	C8
Bertha Peak, second jeep road	R	0.7	278.6	7735	C8
Cougar Crest Trail 1E22		0.4	279.0	7680	C8
Holcomb Valley Road 2N09	R	0.8	279.8	7550	C8
Road 3N12, atop a saddle, junction to Delamar Spring	w,R: 0.90m W	2.8	282.6	7755	C8
Cross dirt road	R	0.8	283.4	7610	C8
Cross jeep road	R	1.1	284.5	7305	C8
Little Bear Springs Trail Camp	w	2.5	287.0	6600	C9
Holcomb Creek	w	0.3	287.3	6510	C9
Reach a saddle		2.1	289.4	6485	C9
Cross a dirt road	R	0.9	290.3	6350	C9
Crab Flats Road 3N16	R	3.5	293.8	5465	C10
Cross Holcomb Creek		0.2	294.0	5430	C10
Cienega Redonda Trail, next to Cienega Redonda fork of Holcomb Creek	w	1.0	295.0	5325	C10
Junction with Hawes Ranch Trail	w	0.4	295.4	5230	C10
Holcomb Crossing Trail Camp	w	0.3	295.7	5190	C10
90 foot steel and wood bridge spanning Deep Creek	w	4.1	299.8	4580	C11
Cedar Glen P.O., 28982 Hook Creek Rd., Cedar Glen, CA 92321, (909) 337-4614	PO,w,G,M,L: 4.30m SW	0.0	299.8	4580	C11
Bacon Flats Road 3N20	R	2.6	302.4	4255	C11
Deep Creek Hot Spring	w	6.8	309.2	3535	C12
Cross Deep Creek via bridge		2.0	311.2	3315	C12
Mojave River Forks Reservoir Dam		3.0	314.2	3131	C13
Deep Creek ford	w	0.5	314.7	2990	C13

Southern California

Landmark	Facilities	Diff	S->N	Elev	Map
Torn-up paved road	R	0.6	315.3	3010	C13
Highway 173	R	0.4	315.7	3190	C13
Little-used jeep road	R	0.4	316.1	3205	C13
Trailside spring	w	1.7	317.8	3470	C13
Jeep road atop a saddle	R	1.5	319.3	3430	C14
Grass Valley Creek	w	0.3	319.6	3330	C14
Steep jeep road	R	0.7	320.3	3480	C14
North-descending jeep road halfway to Silverwood Lake	w,G,R: 0.30m NW	2.6	322.9	3480	C14
Road 2N33	R	2.2	325.1	3400	C14
Poorly paved road	R	0.4	325.5	3170	C14
Highway 173	R	0.3	325.8	3175	C14
Very poor dirt road south of Mojave Siphon Power Plant	R	0.5	326.3	3200	C15
First saddle in Silverwood Lake State Recreation		0.6	326.9	3460	C15
Unsigned spur trail to Garces Overlook		2.5	329.4	3580	C15
Cross jeep road	R	0.8	330.2	3455	C15
Two-lane bike path to Cleghorn Picnic Area	w: 0.50m E	0.7	330.9	3390	C15
Signed junction to group-camp complex		0.1	331.0	3380	C15
Silverwood Lake State Recreation Area's entrance road	w,G,M,sh,R: 1.70m E	0.1	331.1	3390	C15
Offramp, west		0.1	331.2	3395	C15
Small picnic area		0.4	331.6	3440	C15
Narrow paved road to water tank	R	0.4	332.0	3530	C15
Leave SRA and join jeep road	R	2.2	334.2	4040	C15
Road atop viewful Cleghorn Ridge	R	0.3	334.5	4160	C15
Small stream	w	0.9	335.4	3830	C15
Little Horsethief Canyon's dry creek bed		2.8	338.2	3570	C16
Road under a huge power-transmission line	R	2.5	340.7	3840	C17

Southern California

Landmark	Facilities	Diff	S->N	Elev	Map
Cross Road 3N44	R	2.4	343.1	3355	C17
Cross another road	R	0.4	343.5	3300	C17
Descending dirt road	R	0.2	343.7	3265	C17
Better dirt road, end of descent	R	0.3	344.0	3140	C17
Crowder Canyon	w	0.3	344.3	3045	C17
Interstate 15 in Cajon Canyon	w,G,M,L: 0.50m NW	0.4	344.7	3000	C17
	Water Alert (↓):	22.3m			
PCT trail resumes		0.4	345.1	2930	D1
Southern Pacific Railroad tracks		0.8	345.9	3020	D1
Road 3N78, second powerline road	R	1.2	347.1	3360	D1
Swarthout Canyon Road 3N28	R	3.1	350.2	3560	D1
Jeep road	R	0.5	350.7	3700	D1
Sharpless Ranch Road 3N29	R	3.9	354.6	5150	D2
Gap in the ridge		1.0	355.6	5260	D2
Sheep Creek Truck Road 3N31	R	3.2	358.8	6300	D2
Viewpoint on ridge-top flat		0.2	359.0	6350	D2
Roadend just east of Gobber's Knob	R	0.9	359.9	6480	D2
Jeep road atop Blue Ridge	R	4.3	364.2	8115	D3
Posted trailhead		0.1	364.3	8176	D3
Acorn Canyon Trail		1.6	365.9	8250	D3
Wrightwood P.O., CA 92397, (800) 275-8777	PO,w,G,M,L: 4.50m N	0.0	365.9	8250	D3
Mountain Hardware, 1390 Highway 2, P.O. Box 398, Wrightwood, CA 92397, (619) 249-3653	w,G,r,R: 4.50m N	0.0	365.9	8250	D3
Guffy Campground	w: 0.15m N	0.9	366.8	8225	D3
	Water Alert (↑):	22.6m			
Dirt road beside an artificial lake	R	2.3	369.1	8115	D4
PCT pathway on the west side of the reservoir		0.1	369.2	8120	D4
Road 3N06	R	0.4	369.6	7955	D4

Southern California

Landmark	Facilities	Diff	S->N	Elev	Map
Blue Ridge Campground		0.1	369.7	7910	D4
Angeles Crest Highway 2	R	2.2	371.9	7386	D4
Grassy Hollow Family Campground	w	1.0	372.9	7300	D4
Spur to walk-in Jackson Flat Group Campground		1.3	374.2	7480	D5
Road 3N26	R	1.5	375.7	7220	D5
Vincent Gap		0.8	376.5	6585	D5
Side trail to Lamel Spring	w: 0.06m S	1.7	378.2	7765	D5
Mt. Baden-Powell Spur Trail		2.1	380.3	9245	D5
Lateral trail to Lily Spring	w: 0.33m N	3.6	383.9	8540	D6
Windy Gap		1.6	385.5	7588	D6
Little Jimmy Spring	w	0.2	385.7	7460	D6
Little Jimmy Campground		0.2	385.9	7450	D6
Cross Road 9W03	R	1.2	387.1	7360	D6
Angeles Crest Highway 2	R	1.0	388.1	6670	D6
Mt. Williamson Summit Trail		1.6	389.7	7900	D6
Angeles Crest Highway 2	R	1.3	391.0	6700	D6
Eagles Roost Picnic Area		0.9	391.9	6650	D7
Rattlesnake Trail 10W03		1.2	393.1	6165	D7
Little Rock Creek	w	0.3	393.4	6080	D7
Burkhart Trail 10W02 next to Little Rock Creek	w	2.3	395.7	5640	D7
Pass Burkhart Trail		0.3	396.0	5730	D7
Cooper Canyon Trail Campground	w	1.2	397.2	6240	D7
Cloudburst Summit		1.7	398.9	7018	D7
Second highway crossing below a hairpin turn	R	0.9	399.8	6735	D8
Road junction in Cloudburst Canyon	R	0.6	400.4	6545	D8
Camp Glenwood	w	0.8	401.2	6400	D8
Highway 2	R	0.5	401.7	6320	D8
Three Points on Angeles Crest Highway	R	1.9	403.6	5885	D8
Unused dirt road	R	1.5	405.1	5760	D8
Another dirt road leads to Pasadena Camp	R	0.2	405.3	5655	D8

Southern California

Landmark	Facilities	Diff	S->N	Elev	Map
Signed trail junction, hiker's left, horse's right		1.5	406.8	5240	D8
Sulphur Springs Campground	w: 0.20m E	0.1	406.9	5200	D8
Merge with the foot trail		0.5	407.4	5265	D8
Little Rock Creek Road 5N04	R	0.3	407.7	5320	D8
Gap at the head of Bare Mountain Canyon		2.1	409.8	5830	D8
Shaded, seeping spring	w	1.1	410.9	6240	D9
Fountainhead Spring	w	0.5	411.4	6440	D9
Ridgetop vista point		1.4	412.8	6760	D9
Shady gap near Pacifico Mountain Campground		0.8	413.6	6645	D9
Jeep road	R	1.7	415.3	6380	D9
Trail resume		0.5	415.8	6210	D9
Signed spur trail to Pacifico Mountain Road 3N17 trailhead	w,R	3.2	419.0	4980	D9
Mill Creek Summit, Ranger Station	w	0.2	419.2	4910	D9
Cross Mt. Gleason Road	R	2.6	421.8	5590	D10
Road 4N24	R	3.7	425.5	5500	D10
Big Buck Trail Camp		0.8	426.3	5195	D10
Junction with a south-branching trail		3.8	430.1	6360	D11
Mt. Gleason's north ridge		0.1	430.2	6410	D11
Messenger Flats Campground	w	0.8	431.0	5870	D11
Moody Canyon Road	R	1.4	432.4	5320	D11
Santa Clara Divide Road	R	1.3	433.7	5425	D11
PCT trail resumes		0.1	433.8	5395	D11
West-descending jeep track		0.7	434.5	5395	D12
BPL Road 4N32 Nork Fork Saddle Ranger Station	w,R	2.0	436.5	4210	D12
Mattox Canyon creek	w	4.3	440.8	2685	D12
Cross Indian Canyon Road 4N37	R	3.3	444.1	2640	D13
Soledad Canyon Road	R	1.1	445.2	2237	D13
Acton P.O., 3632 Smith Ave., Acton, CA 93510, (800) 275-8777	PO,w,G,M: 5.80m E	0.0	445.2	2237	D13

Southern California

Landmark	Facilities	Diff	S->N	Elev	Map
Santa Clara River ford	w	0.1	445.3	2205	D13
Southern Pacific Railroad tracks		0.1	445.4	2243	D13
Saddle out of the canyon		0.4	445.8	2485	D13
Young Canyon Road	R	1.5	447.3	2960	D13
Gap near the head of Bobcat Canyon		0.7	448.0	2980	D13
Jeep road separating Soledad and Aqua Dulce canyons	R	1.6	449.6	3160	D13
Saddle during the descent		0.5	450.1	2960	D13
Canyon bottom		2.0	452.1	2400	D13
Antelope Valley Freeway 14	R	0.1	452.2	2370	D13
Cross to the canyon's north bank		0.6	452.8	2335	D13
Junction on dirt road, descending west	R	0.5	453.3	2535	D13
Gate at a large parking area		0.1	453.4	2485	D13
PCT trail, perhaps signed by a lone brown plastic PCT post		0.5	453.9	2310	D13
Escondido Canyon Road	R	0.2	454.1	2510	D13
Aqua Dulce Canyon Road	R	0.3	454.4	2470	D13
Darling Road (downtown Aqua Dulce)	w,G,M,R	0.5	454.9	2530	D13
	Water Alert (↓):	22.9m			
Old Sierra Highway	R	1.8	456.7	2725	E2
Mint Canyon Road	R	0.1	456.8	2730	E2
Petersen Road	R	0.1	456.9	2755	E2
Dirt road	R	0.1	457.0	2750	E2
Angeles National Forest boundary		0.4	457.4	2905	E3
Mint Canyon step-across creek		1.3	458.7	2865	E3
Big Tree Trail 14W02		1.1	459.8	3330	E3
Sierra Pelona Ridge Road 6N07	R	2.2	462.0	4500	E3
Up to a low saddle		0.3	462.3	4555	E3
Bear Spring		0.7	463.0	4350	E3
Ridgetop-firebreak jeep trail		0.7	463.7	3995	E3
Junction with the old PCT		1.0	464.7	3785	E3

Landmark	Facilities	Diff	S->N	Elev	Map
trail					
Bouquet Canyon Road 6N05	R	0.5	465.2	3340	E3
Old California Riding and Hiking Trail (CRHT)		2.7	467.9	3985	E3
Pass with another firebreak above Leona Divide Road	R	1.4	469.3	4300	E5
Road 6N09	R	2.0	471.3	3725	E5
Ridge with a firebreak		2.1	473.4	3815	E5
San Francisquito Canyon Road	w,R: 0.15m SW	4.2	477.6	3385	E5
	Water Alert (↑):	22.7m			
Dirt road above San Francisquito Canyon	R	0.3	477.9	3520	E5
Grass Mountain Road	R	1.3	479.2	4275	E5
Saddle where four dirt roads converge	R	1.3	480.5	3900	E6
Tule Canyon Road 7N01	R	1.2	481.7	3900	E6
Elizabeth Lake Canyon Road 7N09	R	3.5	485.2	3050	E6
Lake Hughes P.O., 16817 Elizabeth Lake Rd., Lake Hughes, CA 93532, (800) 275-8777	PO,w,G,M,L,sh, r: 2.20m N	0.0	485.2	3050	E6
Trailside wet-season spring	w	1.2	486.4	3710	E6
	Water Alert (↓):	29.6m			
Sawmill-Liebre Firebreak		0.6	487.0	4190	E6
Maxwell Truck Trail 7N08		1.9	488.9	4505	E7
Cross two dirt roads	R	2.9	491.8	4680	E7
Ascend to a trail intersection with Upper Shake Campground	w: 0.60m N	0.4	492.2	4805	E7
Ridgetop road junction above Shake Canyon	R	2.6	494.8	5245	E7
Ridgenose to a junction with a spur trail to Sawmill Campground		1.8	496.6	5015	E8
Road crossing	R	1.1	497.7	4790	E8
Atmore Meadows Spur Road 7N19	w,R: 1.70m SW	0.5	498.2	4705	E8

Southern California

Landmark	Facilities	Diff	S->N	Elev	Map
Up to a grassy saddle		2.1	500.3	5655	E8
Spur trail to waterless Bear Campground		2.2	502.5	5370	E9
Liebre Mountain Truck Trail 7N23		0.2	502.7	5545	E9
North-descending dirt road	R	0.9	503.6	5580	E9
Jeep road	R	1.2	504.8	5745	E9
Dirt road	R	0.1	504.9	5720	E9
Jeep track ends		1.0	505.9	5140	E9
Levels out at a dirt road spur	R	2.5	508.4	3995	E9
Small pond		0.6	509.0	3810	E9
Pine Canyon Road	R	0.3	509.3	3845	E9
Cross a jeep road	R	3.8	513.1	3522	E10
Over-engineered switchbacks to merge with a good jeep road	R	2.1	515.2	3175	E10
Highway 138	w,R	0.8	516.0	3040	E10
	Water Alert (↓):	16.4m			
	Water Alert (↑):	29.6m			
The Country Store, Star Route 138, 28105 West Avenue C6, Lancaster, CA 93536-9207, (805) 724-9097	w,G,r: 1.00m W	0.0	516.0	3040	E10
Old Lancaster Road, 270th Street West	R	0.5	516.5	2992	E10
Pavement ends		0.3	516.8	2970	E10
Pair of roads that bridge the aqueduct at a siphon	R	1.0	517.8	2965	E10
Los Angeles Aqueduct, turning east		0.3	518.1	2965	E10
Straight-north course turns east		3.2	521.3	3090	E11
Intersection with a good dirt road after Little Oak Canyon Creek	R	5.5	526.8	3110	E12
Ignore dirt road, continue on better road	R	3.0	529.8	2893	E12

Southern California

Landmark	Facilities	Diff	S->N	Elev	Map
Triangular junction		0.4	530.2	2915	E12
Los Angeles Aqueduct, underground		0.6	530.8	3105	E12
Cottonwood Creek bridge	w	1.6	532.4	3120	E12
	Water Alert (↓):	22.5m			
	Water Alert (↑):	16.4m			
Next dirt road	R	0.1	532.5	3120	E12
Resumption of PCT trail		0.4	532.9	3160	E12
Bike path overlooking Cottonwood Creek		0.5	533.4	3250	E12
East-west jeep road	R	1.0	534.4	3465	E12
T junction, poor dirt roads	R	0.5	534.9	3609	E12
Up to a viewful and breezy knoll		0.4	535.3	3800	E13
Poor jeep road that traces the south boundary of a barbed-wire fence	R	0.2	535.5	3790	E13
Join good jeep road	R	0.7	536.2	4070	E13
End of the fence		0.3	536.5	4120	E13
Rough jeep/dirtbike path, west of Tylerhorse Canyon		2.2	538.7	4960	E13
Tylerhorse Canyon		0.3	539.0	4840	E13
Saddle overlooking Gamble Spring Canyon		3.2	542.2	4960	E13
Gamble Spring Canyon		0.7	542.9	4625	E13
Cross a jeep road	R	3.0	545.9	6070	E13
Headwaters of Burnham and Pitney canyons		2.6	548.5	5980	E14
Cross Oak Creek via steel bridge	w	6.4	554.9	4075	E15
	Water Alert (↓):	24.9m			
	Water Alert (↑):	22.5m			
Paved Tehachapi-Willow Springs Road	R	0.2	555.1	4150	E15
Tehachapi P.O., CA 93561, (800) 275-8777	PO,w,G,M,L,r: 11.40m W	0.0	555.1	4150	E15
Mojave P.O., CA 93501, (805) 824-4561	PO,w,G,M,L,r: 12.00m E	0.0	555.1	4150	E15

Southern California

Landmark	Facilities	Diff	S->N	Elev	Map
One good dirt road with plastic marker-posts	R	0.8	555.9	4165	E15
Second dirt road	R	0.2	556.1	4160	E15
Up to a small saddle		0.6	556.7	4495	E15
Viewful ridgetop		0.6	557.3	4560	E15
Fourth, good dirt road	R	1.6	558.9	4485	E16
Down to a saddle with a poor dirt road	R	0.5	559.4	4600	E16
Cross a dirt road	R	0.9	560.3	4765	E16
Cameron Road	R	2.1	562.4	3905	E16
Atchison Topeka and Santa Fe and Southern Pacific Railroad tracks		0.5	562.9	3824	E16
Tehachapi Pass, start of Sierra Nevada		0.8	563.7	3830	E16
Gate opposite the Cameron Road Exit 1 mile sign	R	1.2	564.9	3780	F1
Trail end after the head of Waterfall Canyon		7.1	572.0	6120	F2
0.2 mile from the gated road, after the Sky River Ranch sign	R	4.3	576.3	6000	F3
Golden Oaks Spring	w	3.5	579.8	5480	F4
	Water Alert (↓):	18.3m			
	Water Alert (↑):	24.9m			
Cross a green gate in a cattle fence		6.5	586.3	5102	F5
Cross below a camping area by an east-west road	R	3.0	589.3	5010	F5
Hamp Williams Pass		3.3	592.6	5530	F5
Curve of a private dirt road	R	3.2	595.8	5620	F6
T junction		0.8	596.6	5996	F6
Ascend along a tight right curve, PCT path on left		0.4	597.0	6160	F6
Cross a dirt road leading to Robin Bird Spring	w,R: 0.10m W	1.0	598.0	6360	F7
	Water Alert (↑):	18.2m			
Jawbone Canyon Road	R	0.4	598.4	6620	F7

Southern California

Landmark	Facilities	Diff	S->N	Elev	Map
Log footbridge over branch of Cottonwood Creek	w	1.8	600.2	6480	F7
Logging road	R	1.0	601.2	6720	F7
Landers Creek	w: 0.20m W	1.9	603.1	6300	F7
Piute Mountain Road	R	0.9	604.0	6220	F7
SNF Road 29S05	w,R: 0.30m N	0.7	604.7	6300	F7
	Water Alert (↓):	35.5m			
Piute Mountain Road again, summit of Harris Grade	R	2.3	607.0	6620	F7
Kelso Valley Road at a pass	R	4.8	611.8	4953	F9
Butterbredt Canyon Road, SC123 to a spring	w,R: 1.20m N	2.1	613.9	4540	F9
Slopes of Pinyon Mountain, multi-road-and-path junction to Willow Spring, Road SC103	w,R: 1.80m NW	4.1	618.0	5283	F10
Another multi-road-and-trail junction	R	1.6	619.6	5382	F10
A ridgecrest saddle		1.1	620.7	5700	F10
Road SC328 on a crestline saddle	R	0.8	621.5	5300	F10
Road SC47 on another crestline saddle	R	0.2	621.7	5380	F10
Road SC42	R	3.0	624.7	5740	F10
Junction at Bird Spring Pass		2.5	627.2	5355	F11
Ridge with a westward orientation		2.4	629.6	6460	F11
Highest point before Walker Pass and beyond		1.3	630.9	6940	F11
Road to Yellow Jacket Spring	w,R: 0.70m NW	2.3	633.2	6260	F11
Join the road to McIvers Spring	R	4.5	637.7	6670	F12
Junction to McIvers Spring	w: 0.30m E	2.2	639.9	6680	F12
	Water Alert (↑):	35.5m			
Curve around a sharp canyon crease		3.0	642.9	6680	F13
Ridgeline saddle after Jacks Creek		2.2	645.1	5860	F13

Southern California

Landmark	Facilities	Diff	S->N	Elev	Map
Path leading to Walker Pass Trailhead Campground	w: 0.10m N	2.1	647.2	5100	F13
	Water Alert (↓):	12.4m			
Historical Marker		0.6	647.8	5246	F13
Onyx P.O., CA 93255, (760) 378-2121	PO,w,G,r: 17.60m W	0.0	647.8	5246	F13
Trailside Medium-sized campsite		2.1	649.9	6390	G1
North facing slopes to a saddle		1.8	651.7	6585	G2
Morris/Jenkins saddle		0.8	652.5	6500	G2
Commemorative plaque		0.3	652.8	6580	G2
Rounded point of a ridge		1.3	654.1	6950	G2
Jenkins/Owens saddle		2.2	656.3	7020	G1
A lesser saddle		1.3	657.6	6300	G1
Rough dirt road	R	1.3	658.9	5500	G1
Joshua Tree Spring	w: 0.25m SW	0.4	659.3	5360	G1
	Water Alert (↑):	12.2m			
Cross a ridge at a saddle		1.1	660.4	5240	G1
Northwest to another saddle		1.1	661.5	5860	G3
Branch of Spanish Neddle Creek	w	2.2	663.7	5160	G3
Spring-fed branch of Spanish Neddle Creek	w	0.7	664.4	5300	G3
Spring-fed streamlet	w	0.6	665.0	5560	G3
Spanish Neddle Creek (3rd encounter)	w	0.2	665.2	5620	G3
Ridge between Spanish Needle Group and Lamont Peak		3.0	668.2	6800	G4
Second broader saddle		3.3	671.5	6900	G4
Sierra crest saddle with limited views		1.4	672.9	6260	G4
Seasonal creek		0.8	673.7	5950	G4
Canebrake Road	w,R: 0.30m NE	2.4	676.1	5555	G4
	Water Alert (↓):	12.4m			
Fox Mill Spring		2.0	678.1	6580	G4
Dirt road	R	0.2	678.3	6580	G4
Trail summit		3.6	681.9	8020	G5

Landmark	Facilities	Diff	S->N	Elev	Map
Road crossing	R	0.2	682.1	7980	G5
Long Valley Loop Road	R	1.9	684.0	7220	G5
Spur ridge - last camp before Rockhouse Basin		2.7	686.7	6600	G6
First creek after Rockhouse Basin	w	1.8	688.5	5845	G6
	Water Alert (↑):	12.7m			
Seasonal creek	w	3.2	691.7	5870	G6
South Fork Kern River	w	1.0	692.7	5760	G7
Road junction	R	1.9	694.6	5950	G7
Stream	w	0.1	694.7	5916	G7
Closed OHV road	R	0.6	695.3	5980	G7
Bridge near Kennedy Meadows general store		1.7	697.0	6020	G7
Kennedy Meadows General Store, P.O. Box 3A-5, Inyokern, CA 93527	w,G,r: 0.70m SE	0.0	697.0	6020	G7

Central California

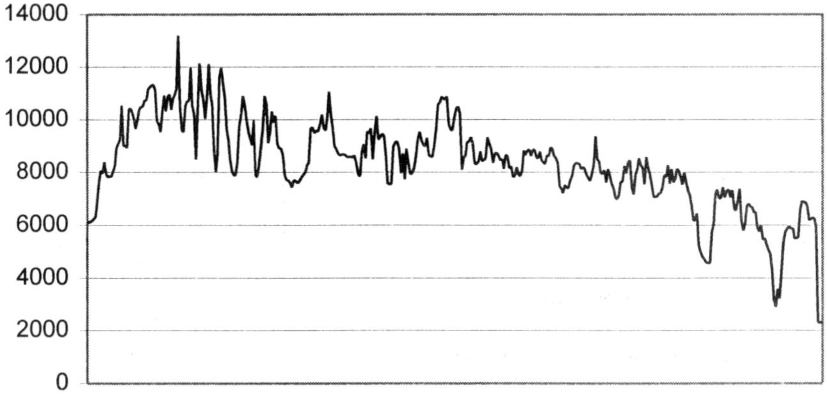

Section Total Mileage: 586.1 miles

Landmark	Facilities	Diff	S->N	Elev	Map
Cross road to campground	R	1.8	698.8	6080	G7
Cross road again	R	0.4	699.2	6120	G7
Kennedy Meadows Campground	w	0.2	699.4	6150	G7
Junction leaving Clover Meadow Trail		1.1	700.5	6240	G8
Steel-girdered wooden bridge	w	0.8	701.3	6300	G8
Crag Creek	w	2.0	703.3	6810	G8
Junction with the old Clover Meadow Trail		2.5	705.8	7560	G8
T junction with Haiwee Trail 37E01		1.1	706.9	8060	G8
Beck Meadows Trail 35E01		0.4	707.3	7953	G8
Deer Mountain's northern ridge		2.2	709.5	8390	G9
Low, broad ridge		1.0	710.5	7940	G9
South Fork Kern River bridge in Monache Mdws.	w	0.4	710.9	7820	G9
Southeast-heading trail to		0.1	711.0	7840	G9

Landmark	Facilities	Diff	S->N	Elev	Map
Kennedy Meadows					
Right turn at a junction		0.1	711.1	7840	G9
Low ridge		1.2	712.3	8050	G9
Cow Creek	w	1.3	713.6	8260	G10
Olancha Pass Trail		1.2	714.8	8920	G10
Trail junction after Cow Creek	w	0.5	715.3	9090	G10
North to a lateral		0.2	715.5	9240	G10
After Monache Creek bowl, levels off on a saddle		3.4	718.9	10540	G10
Cross a year-round creek	w	3.7	722.6	9030	G11
Meadowside trail at a causeway abutment		0.7	723.3	9010	G11
Ford a step-across all-year Death Canyon creek	w	1.7	725.0	8940	G11
Crestline saddle		3.7	728.7	10390	G11
Junction with a faint half mile long lateral to a spring	w: 0.30m N	1.5	730.2	10425	G11
Second saddle with path signed CORRAL	w: 0.20m E	1.6	731.8	10260	G12
Descent northwest to an obscure path		1.8	733.6	10000	G12
Sierra crest at a low saddle to Diaz Creek	w: 0.50m E	1.8	735.4	9670	G12
CORRAL junction sign	w: 0.20m N	1.3	736.7	9960	G12
Mulkey Pass		1.5	738.2	10380	G12
Junction with Trail Pass Trail		0.8	739.0	10500	G12
Lone Pine P.O., 121 E Bush St., Lone Pine, CA 93545, (760) 876-5681	PO,w,G,M,L,r: 24.90m E	0.0	739.0	10500	G12
Path to Poison Meadow		1.3	740.3	10740	G13
Intersect the crest at a saddle		0.6	740.9	10740	G13
Cottonwood Pass		2.9	743.8	11160	G13
Chicken Spring Lake outlet	w	0.6	744.4	11235	G13
Seasonal creek	w	2.5	746.9	11320	G14

Central California

Landmark	Facilities	Diff	S->N	Elev	Map
Sequoia National Park border		0.6	747.5	11320	G14
Siberian Pass/Rock Creek trail		0.9	748.4	11139	G14
Down to a junction with Rock Creek Trail		4.9	753.3	9959	G14
Cross a brook	w	0.3	753.6	9840	G14
Rock Creek crossing	w	0.9	754.5	9550	G15
Guyot Creek	w	1.5	756.0	10320	G15
Pass northeast of 12,300 foot Mt Guyot		1.0	757.0	10920	G15
Crabtree Meadow with lateral to Mt. Whitney	w	3.5	760.5	10329	G15
Path north-northwest to a signed junction with JMT to Mt. Whitney		0.8	761.3	10870	G15
Sandy Meadow to a high saddle		1.7	763.0	10964	H2
Wallace Creek and High Sierra Trail junction	w	1.6	764.6	10390	H2
Ford of Wright Creek	w	1.1	765.7	10790	H2
Shepherd Pass Trail	w	3.5	769.2	10930	H2
Lake South America Trail		0.7	769.9	11160	H2
Forester Pass		4.3	774.2	13180	H3
Center Basin trail	w	4.5	778.7	10500	H3
Vidette Meadow	w	2.8	781.5	9600	H4
Junction up Bubbs Creek canyon		0.7	782.2	9550	H4
Bullfrog Lake junction		1.5	783.7	10530	H4
Kearsarge Pass trails		0.7	784.4	10710	H4
Independence P.O., 101 S. Edwards St., Independence, CA 93526, (760) 878-2210	PO,w,G,M,L,r: 24.00m E	0.0	784.4	10710	H4
Glen Pass		2.3	786.7	11978	H4
Sixty Lakes Trail	w	2.0	788.7	10550	H4
Dollar Lake (unsigned Baxter Pass Trail)	w	2.6	791.3	10230	H4
Woods Creek	w	3.7	795.0	8492	H5
Sawmill Pass Trail	w	3.4	798.4	10370	H5
Pinchot Pass		3.7	802.1	12130	H5

Central California

Landmark	Facilities	Diff	S->N	Elev	Map
Lake Marjorie	w	1.7	803.8	11160	H6
Taboose Pass Trail	w	1.3	805.1	10750	H6
South Fork Kings River Trail	w	1.3	806.4	10050	H6
South Fork Kings River ford	w	2.2	808.6	10840	H6
Mather Pass		3.0	811.6	12100	H7
Upper Palisade Lake	w	2.5	814.1	11000	H7
Lower Palisade Lake	w	1.0	815.1	10600	H7
Deer Meadow	w	3.0	818.1	8860	H8
Middle Fork Kings River	w	3.7	821.8	8020	H9
Bishop Pass Trail	w	3.3	825.1	8710	H9
Helen Lake	w	5.7	830.8	11595	H10
Muir Pass		1.3	832.1	11955	H10
Evolution Creek	w	2.2	834.3	11400	H10
Evolution Lake Inlet	w	2.4	836.7	10850	H10
McClure Meadow	w	4.9	841.6	9650	H11
Evolution Creek crossing	w	2.5	844.1	9210	H12
South Fork San Joaquin River	w	1.0	845.1	8470	H12
Piute Pass Trail	w	3.5	848.6	8050	H12
Florence Lake Trail		1.8	850.4	7890	H13
Muir Trail Ranch, Box 176, Lakeshore, CA 93634	w: 0.20m SW	0.0	850.4	7890	H13
Florence Lake Trail #2		1.7	852.1	8400	H13
Little Senger Creek	w	2.2	854.3	9740	H13
Another trail below Sally Keyes Lakes	w	1.6	855.9	10150	H13
Selden Pass		2.1	858.0	10900	H14
Marie Lake outlet	w	0.9	858.9	10570	H14
Rosemarie Meadow	w	1.6	860.5	10010	H14
Trail junction up East Fork Bear Creek	w	1.4	861.9	9530	H14
Lake Italy Trail	w	1.2	863.1	9300	H14
Old trail below Hilgard Creek	w	2.0	865.1	9040	H14
Bear Ridge trail junction to Mono Hot Springs	w	1.6	866.7	9980	H15
Mono Creek	w	4.6	871.3	7850	H15
Vermillion Valley Resort, c/o Rancheria Garage, Huntington Lake Road ,	w,G,M,L,R: 6.00m W	0.0	871.3	7850	H15

Landmark	Facilities	Diff	S->N	Elev	Map
Lakeshore, CA 93634, (209) 855-6558					
Junction with Mono Pass Trail		1.6	872.9	8270	H15
North Fork Mono Creek	w	1.4	874.3	8940	H15
Re-ford North Fork Mono Creek	w	1.2	875.5	9640	H15
Silver Pass		2.8	878.3	10900	H15
Goodale Pass Trail	w	1.2	879.5	10550	H16
Cascade Valley Trail	w	2.5	882.0	9130	H16
Tully Hole	w	1.1	883.1	9520	H16
Lake Virginia	w	1.9	885.0	10314	H16
Purple Lake	w	2.1	887.1	9900	H16
Trail to Duck Lake	w	2.3	889.4	10150	H16
Deer Creek	w	5.5	894.9	9090	H17
Upper Crater Meadow		2.0	896.9	8920	H18
Mammoth Lakes P.O., CA 93546, (760) 934-2205	PO,w,G,M,L,r: 7.25m NE	0.0	896.9	8920	H18
Last campsite before Reds Meadow	w	0.8	897.7	8660	H18
Boundary Creek	w	2.3	900.0	7910	H18
Abandoned stagecoach road	R	0.7	900.7	7700	H18
Reds Meadow, few supplies	w,G,M,L: 0.30m N	0.0	900.7	7700	H18
Reds Meadow, Rainbow Falls-Fish Valley-Cascade Valley Trail		0.2	900.9	7600	H18
Trail junction by east boundary of Devils Postpile NM		0.5	901.4	7430	H18
Old trans-Sierra Mammoth Trail		1.0	902.4	7710	H18
JMT and PCT diverge		0.6	903.0	7660	H18
Minaret Creek	w	0.6	903.6	7590	H18
Bridge across Middle Fork		1.4	905.0	7680	H18
Permanent stream along Middle Fork	w	1.0	906.0	7810	H19
Another stream	w	1.1	907.1	7910	H19
Junction after a small knoll		0.2	907.3	8000	H19
River Trail		0.5	907.8	8280	H19

Central California

Landmark	Facilities	Diff	S->N	Elev	Map
Agnew Meadows road	w,R	0.9	908.7	8360	H19
Descending ridge before Ritter Range	w	2.8	911.5	9680	H19
Junction with trail over Agnew Pass		2.4	913.9	9710	H19
Middle fork-Clark Lakes Trail		0.8	914.7	9500	H20
De facto trail, pass a lakelet	w	0.3	915.0	9590	H20
River Trail		0.5	915.5	9560	H20
Thousand Island Lake	w	1.0	916.5	9840	H20
Island Pass		1.8	918.3	10200	H20
Obscure junction to Davis Lake		1.0	919.3	9690	H20
Rush Creek Trail	w	0.4	919.7	9600	H20
Marie Lakes Trail		0.8	920.5	10030	H21
Donohue Pass		2.6	923.1	11056	H22
Lyell Fork crossing	w	1.8	924.9	10220	H22
Another Lyell Fork crossing	w	0.8	925.7	9700	H22
Lyell Fork base camp	w	1.4	927.1	9000	H22
Junction to Vogelsang High Sierra Camp	w	2.8	929.9	8880	H22
Rafferty Creek Trail		4.4	934.3	8710	H23
Junction to Tuolumne Meadows Campground		0.7	935.0	8650	H23
Dana Fork of the Tuolumne River	w	0.7	935.7	8690	H23
Tuolumne Meadows P.O., CA 95389, (209) 372-0263	PO,w,G,M,L,sh, r: 0.30m W	0.0	935.7	8690	H23
Tuolumne Lodge's road	R	0.3	936.0	8650	H23
Highway 120	R	0.8	936.8	8595	H23
Fork just beyond a minor gap		0.7	937.5	8590	I1
Soda Springs area		0.1	937.6	8600	I1
Delaney Creek	w	0.8	938.4	8570	I1
Young Lakes Trail		0.4	938.8	8650	I1
Bridge over Tuolemne River	w	2.7	941.5	8310	I2
Junction to McGee Lake		1.1	942.6	7920	I2
Glen Aulin, next to Conness Creek	w	0.2	942.8	7840	I2

Central California

Landmark	Facilities	Diff	S->N	Elev	Map
Forested gap along Cold Canyon creek		2.9	945.7	8800	I3
McCabe Lakes Trail		3.9	949.6	9080	I3
Virginia Canyon Trail	w	1.2	950.8	8540	I3
Forested pass		2.2	953.0	9560	I3
Miller Lake	w	1.4	954.4	9490	I3
Low gap		0.6	955.0	9680	I3
Matterhorn Canyon Trail	w	1.6	956.6	8510	I3
Wilson Creek, last ford	w	3.3	959.9	9500	I4
Benson Pass		1.2	961.1	10140	I4
South shore on Smedberg Lake	w	1.9	963.0	9250	I4
Well-defined gap		0.3	963.3	9340	I4
Meadowy junction to Rodgers Lake		0.7	964.0	9480	I4
Junction to Murdock Lake		0.3	964.3	9390	I5
Ford of Smedberg Lake's outlet	w	0.8	965.1	8720	I5
Benson Lake spur trail	w	2.1	967.2	7560	I5
Benson Lake	w	0.4	967.6	7550	I5
Return to PCT	w	0.4	968.0	7560	I5
Wind-free, sparkling pond	w	2.1	970.1	8970	I5
Seavey Pass	w	0.6	970.7	9150	I5
Highest gap		0.2	970.9	9180	I5
Junction in Kerrick Canyon	w	0.5	971.4	8930	I5
Lower Kerrick Canyon, Bear Valley Trail junction	w	3.7	975.1	7960	I6
North to a shallow gap		1.4	976.5	8720	I6
Stubblefield Canyon creek	w	1.1	977.6	7740	I6
Macomb Ridge pass		2.4	980.0	8910	I7
Tilden Lake Trail signed junction	w	1.0	981.0	8390	I7
Wilma Lake or Wilmer Lake	w	1.5	982.5	7930	I7
Junction with Jack Main Canyon Trail	w	0.3	982.8	7970	I7
Junction east to Tilden Lake	w	1.9	984.7	8160	I8
South end of Grace Meadow	w	3.7	988.4	8630	I8
First trail to Bond Pass		3.1	991.5	9280	I9
Dorothy Lake Pass		1.5	993.0	9550	I9

Central California

Landmark	Facilities	Diff	S->N	Elev	Map
Lake Harriet	w	1.1	994.1	9210	I9
Cascade Creek footbridge	w	0.7	994.8	9040	I9
Junction to West Walker River Trail	w	0.6	995.4	9000	I9
Junction just past a creek after three ponds	w	0.9	996.3	9320	I9
West Fork West Walker River Trail	w	2.0	998.3	8670	I9
West Fork West Walker River bridge, junction by Lower Long Lake	w	0.2	998.5	8610	I9
Another creek	w	1.6	1000.1	8610	I9
Kennedy Canyon creek	w	1.9	1002.0	9060	I10
Closed jeep road	R	1.2	1003.2	9670	I10
Leave jeep road at a switchback	R	1.9	1005.1	10580	I10
Sierra crest		2.3	1007.4	10640	I10
Ridge, highest point after Donohue Pass		0.7	1008.1	10880	I10
Notch on a steep wall		0.7	1008.8	10780	I10
Another crest crossing		0.8	1009.6	10780	I10
Another crest crossing		1.2	1010.8	10870	I10
First creek since Kennedy Canyon	w	1.7	1012.5	9820	I10
Highway 108	R	0.7	1013.2	9620	I10
Trailhead-parking spur		0.2	1013.4	9610	J1
Start switchback		1.7	1015.1	10080	J1
County-line ridge		0.7	1015.8	10420	J1
Top the Sierra crest at a saddle		0.3	1016.1	10500	J1
Junction atop Wolf Creek Lake saddle to Wolf Creek Lake	w: 0.33m S	1.2	1017.3	10250	J1
East Carson River Trail, descend to a small flat	w	5.2	1022.5	8100	J2
Prominent crest saddle, junction to Boulder Lake		3.1	1025.6	8590	J2
Boulder Creek	w	1.6	1027.2	8600	J2

Central California

Landmark	Facilities	Diff	S->N	Elev	Map
Descend to a saddle by Golden Lake		2.3	1029.5	9170	J3
Paradise Valley/Golden Canyon trails, trail intersection beyond Golden		1.2	1030.7	9170	J3
Saddle with view of Peak 9500		0.7	1031.4	9340	J3
Another saddle after Murray Canyon		1.5	1032.9	9080	J3
East fork of Wolf Creek	w	2.0	1034.9	8320	J3
Middle fork of Wolf Creek	w	0.4	1035.3	8310	J3
Multi-branched west fork	w	0.5	1035.8	8400	J3
Sierra Nevada Crest		0.8	1036.6	8800	J3
Wolf Creek Pass	w	1.0	1037.6	8410	J3
Junction by a gully to Asa Lake		0.3	1037.9	8480	J3
Asa Lake's outlet creek	w	0.2	1038.1	8520	J3
Saddle		1.7	1039.8	9330	J4
Junction with Noble Canyon Trail		0.6	1040.4	9110	J4
Noble Lake outlet creek	w	0.6	1041.0	8900	J4
Junction with northern part of Noble Canyon Trail	w	0.9	1041.9	8360	J4
Highway 4 near Ebbetts Pass	R	2.9	1044.8	8700	J4
Sherrold Lake	w	0.6	1045.4	8760	J4
Raymond Meadows Creek	w	3.4	1048.8	8640	J5
Eagle Creek	w	1.1	1049.9	8460	J5
Deep crest saddle		1.3	1051.2	8510	J5
Pennsylvania Creek	w	0.6	1051.8	8140	J5
Sagebrush saddle		1.0	1052.8	8660	J5
Descend to meet Raymond Lake trail		1.5	1054.3	8640	J5
Raymond Lake creek	w	1.0	1055.3	8150	J5
Conspicuous saddle		0.8	1056.1	8230	J5
Pleasant Valley Trail 008		0.6	1056.7	7820	J5
Tributary of Pleasant Valley Creek	w	0.4	1057.1	7860	J5
Saddle leaving the eastern part of Mokelumne		0.5	1057.6	8200	J5

Landmark	Facilities	Diff	S->N	Elev	Map
Wilderness					
Reach a road	R	1.6	1059.2	7900	J5
Car-camping site	w	0.6	1059.8	7860	J5
Blue Lakes Road	R	2.7	1062.5	8090	J6
Saddle southeast of The Nipple		2.4	1064.9	8830	J6
Lost Lakes spur road	w,R	1.8	1066.7	8660	J6
Muddy pond		1.6	1068.3	8830	J6
Summit City Canyon Trail 18E07		0.2	1068.5	8880	J7
Circles a third tiny pond	w	0.8	1069.3	8630	J7
Rejoin TYT near Frog Lake, junction to Winnemucca Lake	w	3.1	1072.4	8860	J7
Junction south of Frog Lake	w	0.1	1072.5	8870	J7
Highway 88, south end of a long parking lot with Carson Pass markers	R	1.1	1073.6	8580	J8
Flat parking area		0.2	1073.8	8550	J8
Pond-blessed saddle	w	1.4	1075.2	8800	J8
Campsite by infant Upper Truckee River	w	0.8	1076.0	8460	J8
Branch right after two cabins	w	0.7	1076.7	8380	J8
Upper Truckee River	w	0.6	1077.3	8310	J8
Second trail from Schneider Camp		1.5	1078.8	8650	J8
Showers Lake	w	0.1	1078.9	8620	J8
Junction with Trail 17E16		1.9	1080.8	8960	J9
Shallow gap		0.2	1081.0	8890	J9
Saddle junction with Sayles Canyon Trail 17E14		1.4	1082.4	8630	J9
Bryan Meadow	w	0.9	1083.3	8540	J9
Second creek crossing by Benwood Meadow	w	1.1	1084.4	8340	J9
Junction after Benwood Meadow to alternate route to Echo Lake Resort		1.8	1086.2	7475	J9
Road 1N03	R	1.0	1087.2	7390	J9
Highway 50	R	0.7	1087.9	7220	J9

Central California

Landmark	Facilities	Diff	S->N	Elev	Map
Echo Lake Resort		1.3	1089.2	7525	J9
Lower Echo Lake	w	0.2	1089.4	7414	J9
Echo Lake Resort P.O., CA 95721, (503) 659-7207	PO,w,G,M,L,r	0.0	1089.4	7414	J9
Junction to a saddle and Triangle Lake		3.1	1092.5	7700	K2
Another trail junction		0.5	1093.0	7865	K2
Lateral trail above Triangle Lake		0.7	1093.7	8250	K2
North-facing-slope junction with second trail to Lake of the Woods		0.5	1094.2	8350	K2
Past a trail above Lake Margery		0.5	1094.7	8340	K2
Past a trail going to Lake Margery		0.2	1094.9	8310	K2
Junction above Lake Aloha		0.6	1095.5	8140	K2
Reach a gully	w	0.5	1096.0	8190	K2
Junction with Rubicon River Trail	w	0.9	1096.9	8120	K2
Heather Lake's northwest shore	w	0.7	1097.6	7900	K2
Cross Susie Lake outlet creek	w	1.1	1098.7	7790	K2
Swampy meadow where the trail forks		0.6	1099.3	7680	K2
Intersection down to Fallen Leaf area		0.5	1099.8	7940	K2
Junction with Trail 17E09 to Gilmore Lake	w	0.6	1100.4	8290	K2
Dicks Pass		2.3	1102.7	9380	K2
Descend to a rocky saddle, reach a junction to Eagle Falls Picnic Area		1.7	1104.4	8500	K2
Reach a spur trail to Dicks Lake		0.2	1104.6	8450	K2
Trail junction above Middle Velma Lake		1.9	1106.5	7965	K3
Trail descending west to		0.3	1106.8	7940	K3

Landmark	Facilities	Diff	S->N	Elev	Map
Camper Flat					
Junction where PCT and TYT splits		1.1	1107.9	8090	K3
Seasonal Phipps Creek	w	1.5	1109.4	7620	K3
High point		2.0	1111.4	8120	K3
Junction to Lake Genevieve		0.9	1112.3	7880	K4
Jeep road atop a forested saddle	R	2.7	1115.0	7570	K4
Richardson Lake's northwest corner	w	0.5	1115.5	7400	K4
Lightly used road by Miller Creek	w,R	1.7	1117.2	7020	K4
McKinney-Rubicon Springs Road	R	0.2	1117.4	7000	K4
Bear lake road	R	1.9	1119.3	7120	K5
Forest Route 3 near Barker Pass		2.4	1121.7	7650	K5
Tahoe City P.O., 950 N Lake Blvd., Tahoe City, CA 96145, (800) 275-8777	PO,w,G,M,L: 12.00m NE	0.0	1121.7	7650	K5
Saddle after a spring-fed gullly		1.6	1123.3	8240	K5
North Fork Blackwood Creek campsites	w	0.8	1124.1	7960	K5
Low knoll with excellent views		2.4	1126.5	8370	K5
Ward Peak maintenance road	R	3.5	1130.0	8470	K6
Five Lakes Creek, Trail 16E04	w	3.1	1133.1	7430	K6
Whiskey Creek Trail 16E06		1.0	1134.1	7170	K6
Tevis Cup Trail		2.1	1136.2	7915	K6
Headwaters of Middle Fork American River	w	0.6	1136.8	8140	K7
Minor gap just outside of Granite Chief Wilderness		0.7	1137.5	8550	K7
Squaw Creek	w	0.4	1137.9	8270	K7
	Water Alert (↓):	15.3m			
Granite Chief Trail 15E23 to Squaw Valley		1.1	1139.0	8170	K7
Painted Rock Trail 15E06		1.5	1140.5	7550	K7

Central California

Landmark	Facilities	Diff	S->N	Elev	Map
Tinker Knob saddle		2.2	1142.7	8590	K7
Round Peak 8374 to a shallower saddle		2.6	1145.3	8170	K8
Roller Pass		2.8	1148.1	7900	K8
Cross one-lane road	R	0.8	1148.9	7520	K8
Road junction to Lake Mary homesites	R	1.0	1149.9	7060	K8
Old Highway 40 near Donner Pass	R	0.2	1150.1	7090	K8
Soda Springs P.O., CA 95728, (503) 426-3082	PO,w,G,M,r: 3.20m W	0.0	1150.1	7090	K8
Parking, junction one-quarter mile south of Interstate 80	w: 0.12m N	3.0	1153.1	7190	K8
	Water Alert (↑):	15.2m			
Junction by a lakelet's west shore	w	0.9	1154.0	7230	L1
Northwest to a road	R	1.0	1155.0	7440	L1
Castle Pass		1.4	1156.4	7910	L1
Peter Grubb Hut	w	0.9	1157.3	7820	L1
Old jeep road	R	2.2	1159.5	8270	L2
Magonigal Camp jeep road	w,R	1.9	1161.4	7580	L2
Reach a knoll		1.1	1162.5	8120	L2
White Rock Creek	w	1.2	1163.7	7630	L2
Road 19N11A	R	0.7	1164.4	7760	L2
Saddle over Jackson Meadow Reservoir		0.8	1165.2	8140	L2
Cross a road on a viewless saddle	R	0.7	1165.9	8060	L3
Ridge saddle at the head of Bear Valley		1.0	1166.9	7830	L3
Tahoe N.F. Road 86, Meadow Lake Road 19N11	w,R	2.1	1169.0	7530	L3
Climbs to a ridge		1.1	1170.1	8000	L3
Logging road	R	2.1	1172.2	7640	L3
Descend to a creek	w	3.6	1175.8	7330	L3
Minor saddle		0.4	1176.2	7135	L4
Cross another good road	R	2.3	1178.5	6740	L4

Central California

Landmark	Facilities	Diff	S->N	Elev	Map
Junction southeast of Pass Creek Loop Road	w,R	1.7	1180.2	6170	L5
Tahoe N. F. Road 07 near Jackson Meadow Reservoir	R	0.4	1180.6	6200	L5
Minor saddle		0.8	1181.4	6450	L5
First (southern) Milton Creek crossing	w	5.5	1186.9	5240	L5
Bridge over Milton Creek	w	0.8	1187.7	4990	L5
Northward down to closed road to Wild Plum Campground	R	1.2	1188.9	4810	L6
Bridge over Haypress Creek	w	0.3	1189.2	4720	L6
Bridge over North Yuba River	w	1.9	1191.1	4600	L6
	Water Alert (↓):	14.7m			
Highway 49 near Sierra City	R	0.4	1191.5	4570	L6
Sierra City P.O., CA 96125, (503) 862-1152	PO,w,G,M,L,r: 1.50m SW	0.0	1191.5	4570	M1
Switchback up to a flume		2.7	1194.2	5720	M1
Switchback tops off on a ridge		0.7	1194.9	6070	M1
Sierra Buttes jeep trail		3.8	1198.7	7150	M1
Ridgecrest trail junction		1.1	1199.8	7350	M1
Down to a gap on a jeep road	R	0.9	1200.7	7010	M1
Packer Lake Saddle		0.6	1201.3	7020	M1
Reach another jeep road that heads to Deer Lake West	R	2.6	1203.9	7430	M2
Summit Lake road	w,R: 0.10m SE	1.8	1205.7	7050	M2
	Water Alert (↑):	14.6m			
Jeep road cuts northeast across the crest	R	1.3	1207.0	7290	M2
Reach a junction to Oakland Pond		0.9	1207.9	7355	M2
County-line crest saddle with a diminutive pond	w: 0.12m E	2.3	1210.2	7050	M2
Cross a jeep road, twice almost touching it	R	1.3	1211.5	7330	M3
Down to a saddle		1.8	1213.3	6630	M3
the "A" Tree, focal point	w,R	0.5	1213.8	6550	M3

Landmark	Facilities	Diff	S->N	Elev	Map
for five roads					
Rise to a saddle after diverging from Cowell Mine Road	R	1.1	1214.9	6920	M3
Saddle south end of McRae Ridge		0.8	1215.7	7380	M3
Descend to a spot near some campsites	w	3.2	1218.9	6150	M3
Leave Section 30 and West Branch Nelson Creek	w	1.3	1220.2	5790	M4
Johnsville-Gibsonville Road	R	1.2	1221.4	6065	M4
South end of Bunker Hill Ridge		3.0	1224.4	6750	M4
Small, unnamed lake just west of the trail below Bunker Hill Ridge	w	1.5	1225.9	6810	M4
Second saddle next to seasonal spring	w	0.7	1226.6	6700	M4
Forested slopes to a road	R	1.9	1228.5	6680	M5
Quincy-LaPorte Road, continue on a level spur road out to a saddle	w,R: 0.25m SE	1.0	1229.5	6474	M5
Cross Road 22N60 at a saddle	R	0.9	1230.4	6510	M5
Recross Road 22N60 at another saddle	R	1.9	1232.3	5900	M5
Cross Bear Wallow Trail at a jeep road	w,R: 0.50m S	1.4	1233.7	5755	M6
Chimney Rock		1.0	1234.7	6000	M6
Black Rock Creek Road 22N56 at a saddle	w,R: 0.25m S	2.1	1236.8	5460	M6
Junction to Fowler Lake		1.2	1238.0	5500	M6
Reach a second road	R	0.3	1238.3	5280	M6
Sawmill Tom Creek Road 23N65Y	R	1.0	1239.3	5060	M6
Almost touch the road at a saddle	R	1.8	1241.1	4910	M7
Cross road known as Dogwood Creek Road, Butte Road, and Road 23N29X	R	1.6	1242.7	4240	M7

Central California

Landmark	Facilities	Diff	S->N	Elev	Map
Switchback to a delicious spring	w	2.3	1245.0	3180	M7
Middle Fork Feather River	w	0.4	1245.4	2900	M7
Deadman Spring saddle		1.4	1246.8	3590	M7
Bear Creek	w	2.1	1248.9	3240	M7
Switchback to another ridge		2.5	1251.4	4250	M7
Seasonal spring	w	2.3	1253.7	5350	M8
Sunny crest saddle		1.4	1255.1	5750	M8
Seasonal Spring just before Lookout Tower	w	0.3	1255.4	5870	M8
Lookout Rock		0.3	1255.7	5955	M8
Road 23N19	R	0.7	1256.4	5870	M8
Road branching north	R	1.3	1257.7	5880	M9
Big Creek Road 33N56	w,R	1.6	1259.3	5505	M9
Final water supply, a creeklet	w	2.4	1261.7	5520	M9
	Water Alert (↓):	12.4m			
Bucks Summit		2.4	1264.1	5531	M9
Path on a shady left where road turns counterclockwise	R	2.6	1266.7	6550	M10
Shallow saddle, meet Spanish Peak road again	R	1.6	1268.3	6920	M10
Trail junction to Gold Lake Trail		1.4	1269.7	6870	M10
Cross a jeep road	R	1.2	1270.9	6880	M10
Descend to a forested saddle		1.0	1271.9	6710	M10
Clear Creek	w	2.2	1274.1	6190	M11
	Water Alert (↑):	12.4m			
Old California Riding and Hiking Trail by a pond	w	0.5	1274.6	6240	M11
Junction with CRHT that descends to Three Lakes		1.0	1275.6	6270	M11
Shady bend on an old fire road	R	0.4	1276.0	6260	M11
Road dead-ends where Belden Trail of PCT begins	R	1.8	1277.8	5900	M11
Western Pacific's two railroad tracks		4.7	1282.5	2310	M11

Central California

Landmark	Facilities	Diff	S->N	Elev	Map
Belden Town		0.6	1283.1	2310	M11
Belden Town Resort, 14785 Belden Town Road, Belden, CA 95915, (530) 283-9662, via UPS only!	w,G,M,L,sh,r	0.0	1283.1	2310	M11

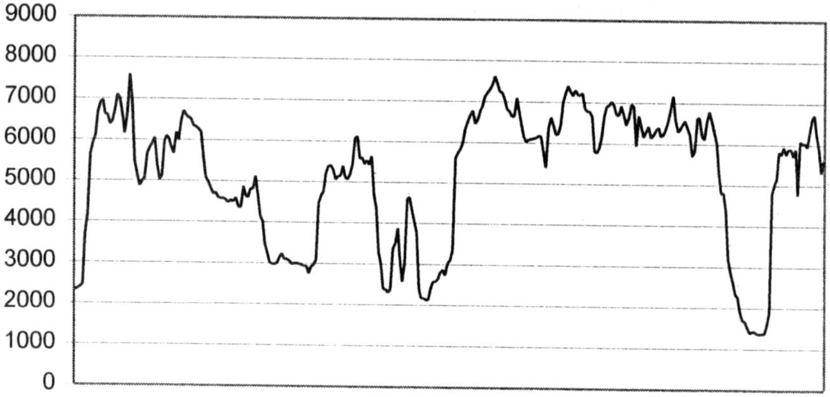

Section Total Mileage: 409.3 miles

Landmark	Facilities	Diff	S->N	Elev	Map
Highway 70 at Belden Town bridge	R	0.1	1283.2	2330	M11
Bridge over Indian Creek	w	1.1	1284.3	2370	N1
Meet a trail after turning west		0.3	1284.6	2400	N1
Junction to an old road	R	0.6	1285.2	2470	N1
Williams Cabin Flat, small cabin on a white-fir-shaded flat	w	4.2	1289.4	3700	N1
Myrtle Flat Camp	w	0.9	1290.3	4180	N2
Creek fed by Poison Spring	w	3.8	1294.1	5650	N3
Junction with an old road	R	0.4	1294.5	5920	N3
Leave old road, forking right	R	0.5	1295.0	6100	N3
Vicinity of Poison Spring headwater	w	1.2	1296.2	6680	N3
Wide lumber road	R	0.4	1296.6	6900	N3
Spring	w	1.0	1297.6	6960	N3
Spur ridge to a roadend	R	1.5	1299.1	6620	N3

Northern California

Landmark	Facilities	Diff	S->N	Elev	Map
Another PCT trail segment		0.7	1299.8	6610	N4
Road 26N02	R	1.0	1300.8	6380	N4
Humbug Road 27N01 at Cold Springs	w,R	1.7	1302.5	6450	N4
Past second road	R	0.7	1303.2	6710	N4
Pond west of the trail	w	1.6	1304.8	7100	N4
North end to a jeep road that levels east to Lost Lake	R	0.9	1305.7	7000	N4
Humboldt Road at Humboldt Summit	R	3.6	1309.3	6610	N5
Descend lowest saddle		3.9	1313.2	6155	N5
Carter Meadow Trail junction	w: 0.50m N	2.3	1315.5	6600	N5
Junction to Butt Mountain summit		3.7	1319.2	7590	N5
Shallow gully		2.6	1321.8	6920	N6
Recross Soldier Creek springs	w	4.2	1326.0	5480	N7
Road after private property	R	1.5	1327.5	5150	N7
Grassy trough		0.7	1328.2	4870	N7
Highway 36	R	1.5	1329.7	4990	N7
Marian Creek, dry most of summer	w	1.6	1331.3	5060	N7
Stover Camp, spring	w	1.6	1332.9	5660	N7
Cross a major road	R	1.1	1334.0	5810	N7
County-line crest		1.4	1335.4	5920	N7
North Stover Mountain		0.7	1336.1	6050	N7
Major logging road on a ridge	R	1.6	1337.7	5400	N8
Bridge over North Fork Feather River	w	1.0	1338.7	5020	N8
Chester-Childs Meadows road	R	0.9	1339.6	5110	N8
Descent northwest to an abandoned road	R	4.1	1343.7	5960	N8
Swampy Little Willow Lake	w	0.7	1344.4	6100	N8
Junction to Terminal Geyser		1.0	1345.4	6030	N8
horse trail		1.8	1347.2	5800	N9
Warner Valley Campground	w	0.9	1348.1	5670	N9
Junction to Bench Lake		1.0	1349.1	6180	N9
Campsites, junction to	w	1.4	1350.5	5990	N9

Northern California

Landmark	Facilities	Diff	S->N	Elev	Map
Summit Lake					
Junction to Horseshoe Lake	w	2.5	1353.0	6470	N9
Second junction that meets the first junction to Horseshoe Lake		1.3	1354.3	6710	N9
Swan Lake outlet creek	w	0.5	1354.8	6620	N9
Trail along Lower Twin Lake, north end	w	0.9	1355.7	6545	N10
Trail descending left		0.4	1356.1	6520	N10
Nobles Trail		2.6	1358.7	6354	N10
Opening with view of Soap Lake		1.0	1359.7	6320	N10
East end of Badger Flat	w	1.6	1361.3	6270	N10
Junction to a horse camp, park's north boundary		2.1	1363.4	6200	N11
Plantation Loop Road	R	1.5	1364.9	5560	N11
East-west road	R	1.7	1366.6	5090	N11
Western arm of the Plantation Loop Road	w,R	0.7	1367.3	4980	N12
Road 32N12	R	1.0	1368.3	4830	N12
Cross a road	R	1.4	1369.7	4690	N12
Atop a faulted escarpment		0.9	1370.6	4720	N12
North-trending road	R	0.8	1371.4	4590	N12
Gate across the road to Hat Creek Resort	R	0.2	1371.6	4580	N12
Old Station P.O., CA 96071, (503) 335-7191	PO,w,G,M,L,sh, r: 0.30m N	0.0	1371.6	4580	N12
Road 32N20	R	0.5	1372.1	4545	N13
Road 32N99	R	0.7	1372.8	4480	N13
Another crossing of Road 32N99	R	0.3	1373.1	4540	N13
Trail fork to Hat Creek Campground		0.4	1373.5	4500	N13
Road 33N22	R	1.3	1374.8	4590	N13
Cross Highway 44 near Subway Cave	w,R: 0.25m W	0.9	1375.7	4365	N13
	Water Alert (↓):	29.4m			
Old Highway 44	R	1.4	1377.1	4360	N13

Northern California

Landmark	Facilities	Diff	S->N	Elev	Map
Highway 44 trailhead	R	1.5	1378.6	4870	N13
Cross usually dry creek gully		1.8	1380.4	4640	N13
Another dry-creek gully		0.9	1381.3	4600	N14
Shallow depression		1.6	1382.9	4820	N14
Another dry-creek gully		2.1	1385.0	4810	N14
Hat Creek Rim Fire Lookout site		4.7	1389.7	5122	N14
Road 22	R	2.8	1392.5	4660	N15
Down to a small reservoir, polluted		1.9	1394.4	4140	N15
Closed gate below Road 36N18	R	3.1	1397.5	4030	N16
Cross Cassel-Fall River Mills Road	R	3.8	1401.3	3480	N17
Cross Conrad Ranch road	R	2.1	1403.4	3270	N17
Road above Rock Spring creek	w,R	1.7	1405.1	3025	N18
	Water Alert (↓):	12.5m			
	Water Alert (↑):	29.7m			
PG&E road south to Cassel	R	0.5	1405.6	2990	N18
Cassel P.O., 21594 Cassel Rd., Cassel, CA 96016, (503) 335-3100	PO,w,G,r: 1.50m SW	0.0	1405.6	2990	N18
Crystal Lake State Fish Hatchery road	R	0.1	1405.7	3000	N18
Cross a jeep road	R	1.5	1407.2	3150	N18
Another jeep road	R	1.8	1409.0	3240	N18
Highway 299	R	0.8	1409.8	3110	N18
Burney P.O., 37116 Main St., Burney, CA 96013, (503) 335-2380	PO,w,G,M,L: 7.00m SW	0.0	1409.8	3110	N18
Slant across a major straight road	R	2.3	1412.1	3070	N18
South edge of Arkright Flat		1.3	1413.4	2995	N18
Cross a nearby road	R	0.4	1413.8	3005	N19
Rim of Lake Road	R	1.2	1415.0	3010	N19
Highway 89	R	1.5	1416.5	2995	N19
large backpacker's camp		0.4	1416.9	2970	N19
Burney Falls, broad path to a parking area on Clark		0.6	1417.5	2950	N19

Landmark	Facilities	Diff	S->N	Elev	Map
Creek Road					
Burney Falls Camp Services, McArthur-Burney Falls State Park, Rte. 1, Box 1240, Burney, CA 96013, (503) 335-4214	w,G,M,sh,r: 0.10m E	0.0	1417.5	2950	N19
	Water Alert (↑):	12.4m			
Lake Britton's dam		1.9	1419.4	2760	O1
Meet a jeep road	R	2.9	1422.3	2930	O2
Rock Creek	w	0.6	1422.9	2980	O2
Road 37N02	R	0.4	1423.3	3100	O2
Cross a road	R	4.3	1427.6	4480	O3
Old clearcut		1.4	1429.0	4660	O3
Peavine Creek	w	2.6	1431.6	4760	O3
Crackling powerlines		1.6	1433.2	5200	O3
Road junction at south base of Red Mountain	R	1.2	1434.4	5380	O3
Road 38N10	R	0.8	1435.2	5410	O3
Another spur road	R	0.7	1435.9	5290	O4
Junction of two roads to Deadman Creek	w,R: 0.50m E	2.1	1438.0	5060	O4
Road 38N10	R	0.2	1438.2	5140	O4
Descend to a logging road	R	1.4	1439.6	5150	O4
Descend to a spot with panoramic view		1.8	1441.4	5390	O4
Cross a descending road down to a pond	w,R: 0.50m SE	2.2	1443.6	5110	O4
Back to Road 38N10, just before Bartle Gap	w,R: 0.15m N	1.6	1445.2	5070	O4
Cross Road 39N90	R	0.4	1445.6	5190	O4
Springs at Moosehead Creek's headwaters	w	1.3	1446.9	5440	O5
Rocky point with a view		2.3	1449.2	6080	O5
Cross Road 38N10	R	1.4	1450.6	6120	O5
Tate Creek, resume at a junction with Road 38N10	w,R: 0.50m N	1.1	1451.7	5580	O5
Recross Road 38N10	R	1.5	1453.2	5610	O6
Alder Creek Trail	w: 0.33m N	1.1	1454.3	5440	O6

Northern California

Landmark	Facilities	Diff	S->N	Elev	Map
Grizzly Peak Road before Pigeon Hill	R	2.1	1456.4	5540	O6
Recross Grizzly Peak Road	R	0.6	1457.0	5420	O6
South ridge of Grizzly Peak Lookout road	R	2.6	1459.6	5640	O6
Deer Creek	w	2.1	1461.7	4700	O7
Side canyon with refreshing creek	w	1.4	1463.1	4360	O7
Butcherknife Creek	w	3.2	1466.3	3300	O7
Dry Doodlebug Gulch		2.1	1468.4	3000	O7
McCloud-Big Bend Road	w,R	1.3	1469.7	2404	O7
Ash Camp	w	0.2	1469.9	2390	O8
Fitzhugh Gulch Creek	w	2.1	1472.0	2320	O8
Ah-Di-Na Campround road, Road 38N53	R	0.4	1472.4	2400	O8
Bald Mountain Road	R	3.1	1475.5	3380	O8
Climb to another road	R	0.8	1476.3	3520	O8
top a ridge saddle		1.9	1478.2	3880	O8
Trough Creek	w	2.1	1480.3	3030	O9
Squaw Valley Creek	w	3.2	1483.5	2580	O9
Southwest to a deep saddle		0.9	1484.4	3059	O9
Girard Ridge Road	R	4.8	1489.2	4600	O10
Northwest-descending ridge		1.8	1491.0	4640	O10
Switchback on a prominent ridge		1.8	1492.8	4330	O10
Fall Creek	w	1.3	1494.1	4050	O10
Cross a road and enter Castle Crags State Park	R	1.5	1495.6	3770	O11
Reach a closed road	R	3.2	1498.8	2420	O11
Paved Riverside Road	R	0.9	1499.7	2180	O11
Castella P.O., CA 96017, (503) 235-4413	PO,w,G,sh,r: 2.00m SW	0.0	1499.7	2180	O11
Interstate 5 near Castle Crags State Park, locked gate		0.7	1500.4	2130	O11
Dunsmuir P.O., 5530 Dunsmuir Ave., Dunsmuir, CA 96025, (503) 235-2507	PO,w,G,M,L: 4.50m N	0.0	1500.4	2130	P1

Northern California

Landmark	Facilities	Diff	S->N	Elev	Map
Junction with Kettlebelly Trail		0.5	1500.9	2420	P1
Root Creek trail	w: 0.25m N	1.3	1502.2	2590	P1
Leave Root Creek Trail		0.1	1502.3	2590	P1
Powerline saddle		0.1	1502.4	2650	P1
Bobs Hat Trail		0.5	1502.9	2820	P1
Winton Canyon creek	w	1.0	1503.9	2875	P1
Sulphur Creek	w	3.1	1507.0	2750	P2
Dog Trail		0.6	1507.6	3040	P2
North Fork tributary	w	1.8	1509.4	3110	P2
Section 31 tributary of North Fork Castle Creek, water upstream	w	1.0	1510.4	3370	P2
Forested saddle just beyond north boundary of Castle Crags State Park		3.6	1514.0	5620	P2
Cascading creek	w	0.4	1514.4	5750	P2
Densely vegetated creeklet	w	1.0	1515.4	5840	P2
West over to crest saddle 5983, water about 0.5m NW cross-country	w: 0.50m NW	0.7	1516.1	5983	P2
Ridge		2.0	1518.1	6320	P2
Soapstone Trail		0.5	1518.6	6500	P2
Peak 6835's south ridge		0.5	1519.1	6670	P2
Trinity Divide	w: 0.33m E	3.7	1522.8	6780	P4
Road 40N30	w,R: 0.33m E	2.3	1525.1	6460	P4
Road 40N45	R	0.8	1525.9	6550	P4
Major saddle		2.1	1528.0	6770	P4
Spring	w	0.4	1528.4	6880	P4
East-dropping ridge with view of Lake Siskiyou		1.8	1530.2	7130	P5
Junction to beautiful Porcupine Lake	w: 0.25m W	0.5	1530.7	7220	P5
Climbs to a crest, junction to Toad Lake		0.3	1531.0	7300	P5
Trail 6W06		0.9	1531.9	7420	P5
Minor gap on the east ridge		0.9	1532.8	7620	P5
Trail intersection on a		1.2	1534.0	7440	P5

Landmark	Facilities	Diff	S->N	Elev	Map
windy saddle					
Spur trail to Deadfall Lake	w	2.1	1536.1	7250	P5
Cross Deadfall Lakes Trail		0.3	1536.4	7230	P5
Gully with a permanent spring	w	1.4	1537.8	7080	P5
Parks Creek Road 42N17, shallow crest saddle	R	1.6	1539.4	6830	P6
Cross an old trail by a small meadow's edge		3.0	1542.4	6770	P6
Tops out on an adjacent ridge		1.6	1544.0	6650	P6
Chilcoot Creek, spring fed creeklet nearby	w	1.7	1545.7	6650	P6
Bull Lake crest saddle, meet old Sisson-Callahan Trail		2.1	1547.8	7100	P6
Secondary crest saddle		1.6	1549.4	6770	P7
Two trail junctions, Little Trinity River Trail 7W01 and Sisson Trail		0.9	1550.3	6480	P7
Next saddle after Peak 6857		1.3	1551.6	6160	P7
Descend to another saddle		0.9	1552.5	6030	P7
Meet two springs	w	1.3	1553.8	6080	P8
Cross a secondary ridge		1.1	1554.9	6100	P8
Masterson Meadow trail	w	0.7	1555.6	6110	P8
Grouse Creek Trail		0.2	1555.8	6130	P8
Masterson Meadow Lake seasonal creek	w	1.1	1556.9	6180	P8
Rocky knoll on a ridge		1.3	1558.2	6170	P8
Trail switchbacks		1.3	1559.5	5790	P8
Highway 3 at Scott Mountain Summit	w,R: 0.25m S	0.6	1560.1	5401	P8
Enter Trinity Alps Wilderness		2.8	1562.9	6370	P9
Shallow crest gap		1.1	1564.0	6630	P9
Spring	w	0.8	1564.8	6440	P9
Road 40N63	R	1.2	1566.0	6210	P9
Mosquito Lake creek	w	0.2	1566.2	6240	P9
Summer camp's primitive trail		0.5	1566.7	6460	P9
Junction to E. Boulder Lake/Marshy Lakes		1.5	1568.2	7020	P1
Edge of talus slope		1.3	1569.5	7240	P9

Northern California

Landmark	Facilities	Diff	S->N	Elev	Map
East end of a windswept crest		0.9	1570.4	7400	P9
Another meadow, spring-fed creeklet	w	0.4	1570.8	7260	P10
North end of a crest saddle, junction with Bloody Run Trail 8W04		0.9	1571.7	7160	P10
On the crest with view of West Boulder Creek canyon		0.6	1572.3	7300	P10
Sage-covered crest saddle		0.4	1572.7	7190	P10
Junction with Trail 8W05		1.2	1573.9	7170	P10
Crest, junction with Trail 8W07 near Section Line Lake		0.3	1574.2	7230	P10
Swath of alders	w	1.4	1575.6	6850	P10
Crest saddle with trail 9W01		1.2	1576.8	6780	P11
Saddle's west end, another branch of Trail 9W01		0.1	1576.9	6780	P11
Narrow crest		0.5	1577.4	6660	P11
South Fork Lakes Trail 9W13		1.5	1578.9	5810	P11
South Fork Scott River	w	0.2	1579.1	5780	P11
Alder-lined creeklet	w	0.5	1579.6	5880	P11
Forest Highway 93 at Carter Meadows Summit	R	0.4	1580.0	6160	P11
Crest saddle with views of South Fork Lakes canyon		1.1	1581.1	6660	P11
Under a crest saddle		1.7	1582.8	6910	P11
Climb to a jeep trail		2.3	1585.1	6940	P13
Jeep trail to Siphon Lake	w: 0.75m W	0.2	1585.3	7030	P13
Bingham Lake's outlet creek under boulders		1.8	1587.1	6940	P13
Alder-choked creek	w	2.3	1589.4	6700	P13
Blakes Fork creek under boulders		0.5	1589.9	6700	P13
Curve northeast, 250 feet below Statue Lake, water from creek	w	1.1	1591.0	6930	P13
Trail 9W09		1.1	1592.1	6710	P14
Paynes Lake Creek	w	2.2	1594.3	6460	P14
Glacial bowl	w	0.7	1595.0	6620	P14

Northern California

Landmark	Facilities	Diff	S->N	Elev	Map
Junction to Taylor Lake		1.5	1596.5	6970	P14
Jeep-road junction to Upper Ruffey Lake	R	2.0	1598.5	6910	P14
Somes Bar-Etna Road at Etna Summit	R	1.7	1600.2	5960	P14
Southeast end of Razor Ridge		3.7	1603.9	6690	Q1
Cross a more persistent creeklet	w	1.0	1604.9	6450	Q1
Reach another creek	w	2.0	1606.9	6170	Q2
Headwaters of Babs Fork Kiddler Creek		0.9	1607.8	6290	Q2
Saddle just north of Peak 6667		1.4	1609.2	6430	Q2
Shelly Lake's outlet creek	w	1.7	1610.9	6150	Q2
Junction with Shelly Meadows Trail		0.3	1611.2	6220	Q2
Shelly Fork Trail/Shelly Meadows Trail		0.2	1611.4	6340	Q2
Saddle below Peak 7109		2.2	1613.6	6410	Q3
Creeklet with campsites	w	0.3	1613.9	6190	Q3
Fisher Lake	w	0.4	1614.3	6220	Q3
Marten Lake	w	0.3	1614.6	6360	Q3
Junction to older PCT route to Kidder Lake Trail		1.2	1615.8	6560	Q3
Conspicuous saddle		0.5	1616.3	6870	Q3
Junction with older PCT segment		1.1	1617.4	7180	Q3
Saddle, meet Shackleford Creek Trail		1.7	1619.1	6590	Q4
Junction to Red Rock Valley Trail/Cold Springs	w: 0.25m S	1.6	1620.7	6310	Q5
Second set of trails to Red Rock Valley Trail/west Cold Spring Trail	w: 0.30m S	0.3	1621.0	6370	Q5
Shadow Lake Trail		0.3	1621.3	6480	Q5
Soft Water Spring	w	0.6	1621.9	6580	Q5
Junction to Sky High Valley trail		0.9	1622.8	6400	Q5

Northern California

Landmark	Facilities	Diff	S->N	Elev	Map
Junction to Big Elk Lake		0.5	1623.3	6232	Q5
Marble Valley Guard Station/Canyon Creek Trail	w	1.0	1624.3	5700	Q5
Marble Gap Trail, water nearby	w	0.3	1624.6	5840	Q5
Junction to Big Rock Camp		2.2	1626.8	6640	Q5
Jumpoff, a low point on a narrow crest		0.4	1627.2	6650	Q5
Notch in southwest end of Cayenne Ridge		2.2	1629.4	6190	Q6
Paradise Lake	w	0.2	1629.6	6130	Q6
Junction to Bear Lake/Turk Lake		1.6	1631.2	6580	Q6
Big Ridge Cutoff Trail, views		0.7	1631.9	6800	Q6
Buckhorn Spring	w	3.3	1635.2	6570	Q6
Small flat with tiny pond	w	0.3	1635.5	6300	Q7
Huckleberry Mountain Trail		1.0	1636.5	6020	Q7
Cross a good road	R	1.5	1638.0	5300	Q7
Cross another good road	R	1.0	1639.0	4800	Q7
Abandoned road	R	1.0	1640.0	4820	Q7
Last logging road crossing	R	0.9	1640.9	4370	Q7
Grider Creek Trail at Road 46N72/Cold Spring creek	w,R	2.0	1642.9	3200	Q7
Footbridge across Grider Creek	w	0.8	1643.7	2870	Q7
Second footbridge across Grider Creek	w	1.3	1645.0	2640	Q7
Third footbridge across Grider Creek	w	1.7	1646.7	2330	Q8
Bark Shanty Creek	w	0.4	1647.1	2280	Q8
Junction with Old Grider Creek Trail	w	1.8	1648.9	1920	Q8
Grider Creek Trail at Grider Creek Campground	w	1.6	1650.5	1700	Q8
Road 46N66	R	0.3	1650.8	1680	Q8
Last bridge across Grider Creek	w	0.8	1651.6	1520	Q8
Junction with a spur road	R	1.5	1653.1	1400	Q9

Northern California

Landmark	Facilities	Diff	S->N	Elev	Map
Highway 96	R	2.4	1655.5	1435	Q9
Klamath River		0.5	1656.0	1430	Q9
Highway 96 at Seiad Valley	R	1.0	1657.0	1371	Q9
Seiad Valley P.O., CA 96086, (503) 496-3211	PO,w,G,M,r	0.0	1657.0	1371	Q9
School House Gulch		0.5	1657.5	1380	R1
Lower Devils Peak Lookout Trail 12W04		0.3	1657.8	1380	R1
Junction to a trail paralleling Highway 96	R	0.2	1658.0	1600	R1
Fern Spring	w	0.7	1658.7	1900	R1
Lookout Spring	w	4.6	1663.3	4800	R1
Lower Devils Peak saddle		0.2	1663.5	5020	R1
Darkey Creek Trail		0.6	1664.1	5170	R1
Upper Devils Peak's western arm		1.0	1665.1	5820	R1
Portuguese Creek Trail 12W03		1.2	1666.3	5760	R1
Boundary Trail 12W47		0.3	1666.6	5940	R1
Spring in spongy ground	w	0.8	1667.4	5760	R1
Kangaroo Mountain's east ridge		0.5	1667.9	5900	R1
Spur trail to a jeep road	R	0.2	1668.1	5900	R1
Cross the jeep road	R	1.0	1669.1	5710	R1
Junction with Horse Camp Trail 958 to Echo Lake		0.5	1669.6	5900	R1
Cook and Green Pass	w: 0.10m NW	2.5	1672.1	4770	R2
Trail 11W02		2.8	1674.9	6080	R2
Horse Creek Trail 11W01		2.2	1677.1	6040	R2
Junction to Lowdens Cabin site	w: 0.12m SE	0.3	1677.4	6040	R3
Junction with the old PCT	w: 0.10m SW	2.0	1679.4	5950	R3
Road 47N81	R	2.4	1681.8	6310	R3
Junction to Buckhorn Camp, Alex Hole Camp entrance	w: 0.30m S	3.1	1684.9	6630	R4
Mud Springs spur road	w,R: 0.20m NW	2.3	1687.2	6730	R5
Road 40S01	R	1.6	1688.8	6250	R5
Road north of Bearground Spring	w,R	0.8	1689.6	5930	R5

Northern California

Landmark	Facilities	Diff	S->N	Elev	Map
Wards Fork Gap		1.3	1690.9	5317	R5
Bridge over Donomore Creek	w	1.5	1692.4	5600	R5

Oregon

Landmark	Facilities	Diff	S->N	Elev	Map

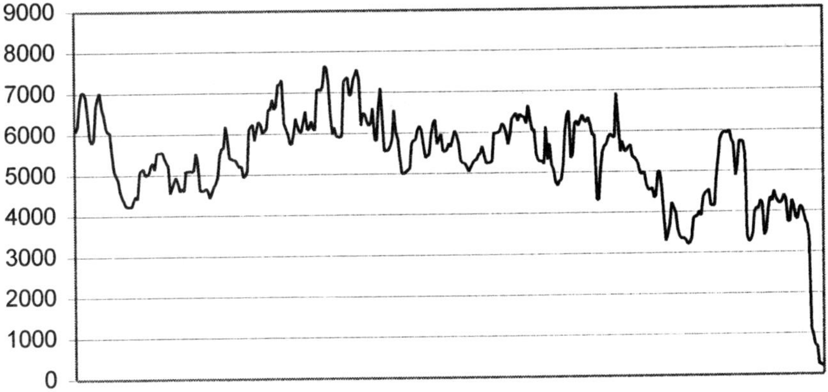

Section Total Mileage: 457.9 miles

Landmark	Facilities	Diff	S->N	Elev	Map
California-Oregon Border		1.3	1693.7	6080	R6
Logging road saddle, cross Road 2025	R	0.1	1693.8	6210	R6
West ridge of twin topped Observation Peak		1.6	1695.4	6750	R6
Observation Gap		1.2	1696.6	7030	R6
Jackson Gap		1.2	1697.8	7040	R6
Spur road to Sheep Camp Spring	w,R	0.3	1698.1	6920	R6
	Water Alert (↓):	12.9m			
Wrangle Gap		2.3	1700.4	6496	R7
Siskiyou Gap		3.8	1704.2	5890	R8
Cross Road 40S12	R	0.3	1704.5	5800	R8
5-way road junction on Long John Saddle	R	1.3	1705.8	5880	R8
Open crest saddle		2.1	1707.9	6710	R8
Cross a spur road	R	0.8	1708.7	6900	R8
Another saddle		1.1	1709.8	7030	R9

Oregon

Landmark	Facilities	Diff	S->N	Elev	Map
Grouse Gap, Road 40S30	w,R: 0.20m S	1.0	1710.8	6630	R9
	Water Alert (↑):	12.7m			
Cross Road 40S15 to Mt. Ashland Campground	w,R: 0.50m NE	1.9	1712.7	6480	R9
Cross Road 20	R	1.5	1714.2	6160	R9
Road 2080	R	0.4	1714.6	6060	R9
Ashland P.O., 120 N 1st St., Ashland, OR 97520, (541) 482-3986	PO,w,G,M,L: 12.40m N	0.0	1714.6	6060	R9
Saddle below the Ashland Inn, water at the Inn	w	1.5	1716.1	5490	R10
Another saddle		0.8	1716.9	5110	R10
Another saddle with 4 roads	R	0.8	1717.7	4990	R10
Spring-fed gully	w	2.1	1719.8	4880	R10
Road past a spring fed gully	R	0.4	1720.2	4610	R10
Cross another road	R	0.1	1720.3	4470	R10
Cross a third road	R	0.1	1720.4	4360	R10
Path ends at abandoned segment of old Highway 99	R	0.8	1721.2	4250	R10
Highway 99, just below Interstate 5 near Mt. Ashland Road 20	R	0.3	1721.5	4240	R10
Callahan's Restaurant and Country Store, 0.9m N	w,G,M: 0.90m N	0.0	1721.5	4240	R10
Ashland P.O., 120 N 1st St., Ashland, OR 97520, (541) 482-3986	PO,w,G,M,L: 12.90m N	0.0	1721.5	4240	R10
Resumption of PCT after I-5		0.5	1722.0	4380	B1
Reach a spring	w	0.9	1722.9	4490	B1
Major intersection		1.3	1724.2	4420	B1
Atop a broad saddle		1.7	1725.9	5080	B1
Cross upper Pilot Rock Jeep Road	R	0.2	1726.1	5120	B1
Reach the first gate		0.9	1727.0	5160	B1
Crest saddle		0.7	1727.7	4990	B1
North to a crest		1.2	1728.9	5020	B2
Trail's resumption on our left		0.2	1729.1	5040	B2

Landmark	Facilities	Diff	S->N	Elev	Map
Cross the jeep road a second time	R	0.8	1729.9	5270	B2
Very refreshing fenced-in spring	w	1.2	1731.1	5290	B2
Descend northeast to a saddle		0.3	1731.4	5140	B2
South slope of Little Pilot Peak		0.9	1732.3	5550	B2
Dips to north side of a saddle		0.1	1732.4	5550	B2
Spring-fed tub, 80 yards northwest down from the trail	w	0.8	1733.2	5550	B2
Meet an old trail		0.2	1733.4	5560	B2
Shaded saddle		0.6	1734.0	5420	B2
Soda Springs Road	R	0.5	1734.5	5300	B3
Hobart Bluff spur trail		0.9	1735.4	5220	B3
Highway 66 at Green Springs Summit	w,R: 0.25m NE	3.4	1738.8	4551	B3
Road 100-90	R	1.4	1740.2	4700	B5
Greensprings Mountain Road	R	0.5	1740.7	4840	B5
Cross a spur road	R	0.7	1741.4	4940	B4
Water faucet (may be gone), fed by an uphill spring	w	0.6	1742.0	4800	B4
Ashland lateral canal, dry gully		0.5	1742.5	4600	B4
Second gully meets a trail to Little Hyatt Reservoir	w: 0.25m N	0.9	1743.4	4670	B5
Hyatt Lake Recreation Road 100-90	R	0.2	1743.6	4610	B5
Hyatt Lake Campground spur trail, past old roads to a road fork	R	1.5	1745.1	5090	B5
Hyatt Lake Resort, 7979 Hyatt Prairie Road, Ashland, OR 97520, (541) 482-3331, via UPS only!	w,G,M,sh,r,R: 0.75m N	0.0	1745.1	5090	B5
Road 39-3E-15	R	2.1	1747.2	5100	B5
Wildcat Glades Road 39-3E-11	R	0.9	1748.1	5090	B5

Oregon

Landmark	Facilities	Diff	S->N	Elev	Map
Cross an older road to Wildcat Glades and reach a seeping creek	R	0.2	1748.3	5100	B5
Reaches the main summit		1.0	1749.3	5540	B5
Almost touch a saddle		0.5	1749.8	5310	B6
Cross a road that climbs southwest to a rock quarry	R	2.0	1751.8	4620	B6
Junction to Soda Creek	w: 0.50m S	0.1	1751.9	4620	B6
Secondary road climbs east	R	0.2	1752.1	4620	B6
Cross a little-used road to Klum Landing Campground	w,R: 0.30m E	0.9	1753.0	4670	B6
Drops northeast to a well-maintained road	R	0.2	1753.2	4610	B6
Grizzly Creek	w	0.5	1753.7	4440	B6
Moon Prairie Road	R	0.4	1754.1	4580	B6
Keno Access Road	R	0.8	1754.9	4720	B6
Old road before the newer logging road	R	0.2	1755.1	4790	B6
Brush Mountain Road	R	0.6	1755.7	4960	B7
Old logging road	R	1.5	1757.2	5480	B7
Approach Griffin Pass Road 2520	R	0.5	1757.7	5640	B7
Parallel Road 2520 to a crossing, east to Big Springs creeklet	w,R: 0.10m E	0.2	1757.9	5670	B7
Rogue River National Forest boundary		1.7	1759.6	6190	B7
Faint spur trail to Road 650	R	1.0	1760.6	5880	B8
Cross a closed road	R	1.2	1761.8	5390	B8
Cross Road 3802	R	0.3	1762.1	5390	B8
Dead Indian Road	R	1.9	1764.0	5360	B8
Junction to South Branch Mountain Shelter	w: 0.10m W	1.5	1765.5	5360	B8
Cross Road 740	R	0.4	1765.9	5270	B8
South Fork Little Butte Creek		2.2	1768.1	5180	B9
Minor ridge		1.4	1769.5	5210	B9
Fish Lake Trail 1014	w: 0.33m W	5.8	1775.3	4940	B9
Highway 140 near Fish Lake	R	0.2	1775.5	4980	B9

Oregon

Landmark	Facilities	Diff	S->N	Elev	Map
Junction to large trailhead parking lot	w	0.3	1775.8	5100	C1
Mt. McLoughlin Trail 3716		4.0	1779.8	6110	C1
Freye Lake spur trail	w: 0.25m N	0.2	1780.0	6190	C1
Leave Mt. McLoughlin Trail, westbound		0.2	1780.2	6240	C1
Twin Ponds Trail to Summit Lake	w: 0.40m NW	3.7	1783.9	5840	C3
Cat Hill Way Trail 992		1.6	1785.5	6100	C3
Broad saddle		1.6	1787.1	6300	C4
Another saddle, junction to Christi's Spring	w: 0.03m N	1.2	1788.3	6240	C4
Red Lake Trail 987		1.1	1789.4	6020	C4
No Name Trail		2.7	1792.1	6070	C5
Sky Lakes Trail 3762		1.0	1793.1	6140	C5
Spur trail to overlook		2.5	1795.6	6600	C5
Wickiup Trail 986/3728		1.0	1796.6	6585	C5
Divide Trail 3717		1.2	1797.8	6840	C5
Hemlock Lake Trail 985		1.0	1798.8	6600	C5
Snow Lakes Trail 3739	w: 0.20m NE	0.2	1799.0	6670	C6
Devils Peak Trail 984		1.7	1800.7	7210	C6
Abandoned segment of Devils Peak Trail		0.2	1800.9	7190	C6
Devils Peak/Lee Peak saddle		0.5	1801.4	7320	C6
Junction to Seven Lakes Trail 981		2.4	1803.8	6250	C6
Sevenmile Trail 3703		0.7	1804.5	6130	C6
Honeymoon Creek	w	0.5	1805.0	5980	C6
Leave Sevenmile Trail		2.1	1807.1	5760	C7
Meet Middle Fork Basin Trail to Ranger Springs	w: 0.90m SW	0.2	1807.3	5750	C7
Junction with Big Bunchgrass Trail 1089A		1.0	1808.3	6020	C7
McKie Camp Trail 1089		0.9	1809.2	6380	C7
Jack Spring spur trail	w: 0.50m NW	2.7	1811.9	6190	C7
	Water Alert (↓):	15.5m			
Abandoned Dry Creek Trail 3701		2.4	1814.3	6040	C8

Oregon

Landmark	Facilities	Diff	S->N	Elev	Map
South end of Stuart Falls Trail 1078		0.2	1814.5	6050	C8
Second old, closed road	R	5.6	1820.1	6290	C8
Top of narrow, open flat		2.4	1822.5	6550	C8
Highway 62, close to Mazama Campground	w,G,sh,R: 1.30m E	2.8	1825.3	6108	C9
Crater Lake National Park P.O., OR 97604, (541) 460-3762	PO,w,G,M,L,r: 4.50m NE	0.0	1825.3	6108	C9
Second fault-line gully		0.8	1826.1	6310	C9
Descend to a closed road	R	0.6	1826.7	6130	C9
Dutton Creek	w	0.7	1827.4	6080	C9
	Water Alert (↑):	16.0m			
Crater Lake Rim Village Junction		2.4	1829.8	7075	C10
Crater Lake Lodge, 400 Rim Village Drive, Crater Lake, OR 97604, (541) 594-2511, Via UPS Only!	w,G,M,L	0.0	1829.8	7075	C10
	Water Alert (↓):	25.9m			
Discovery Point		1.5	1831.3	7050	C9
Junction to Lightning Spring	w: 0.75m W	0.8	1832.1	7150	C9
Junction to The Watchman		1.0	1833.1	7650	C11
Saddle with Overlook		0.2	1833.3	7600	C11
Junction with North Rim access road	R	2.3	1835.6	7253	C12
Junction with PCT equestrian route		3.0	1838.6	6510	C12
Walk east to a road fork and branch northeast	R	2.9	1841.5	5985	C13
Back on trail tread		1.3	1842.8	6150	C13
North boundary of Crater Lake National Park		2.7	1845.5	5942	C13
Highway 138 near the Cascade crest	R	1.9	1847.4	5920	C13
South end of North Crater Trail 1410		0.1	1847.5	5910	D1
Old, abandoned Summit Rock	R	0.5	1848.0	5935	D1

Oregon

Landmark	Facilities	Diff	S->N	Elev	Map
Road					
Mt. Thielsen Trail		5.3	1853.3	7260	D3
New Mt. Thielsen Trail 1456		0.3	1853.6	7330	D3
Head to northwest ridge		1.0	1854.6	7370	D3
Thielsen Creek	w	1.1	1855.7	6930	D3
	Water Alert (↓):	16.5m			
	Water Alert (↑):	25.9m			
Thielsen Creek Trail 1449		0.1	1855.8	6960	D3
Junction with Howlock Mountain Trail 1448		3.1	1858.9	7320	D3
Climb to a crest saddle		0.4	1859.3	7435	D4
Highest point in Oregon-Washington PCT segment		1.3	1860.6	7560	D4
Northeast of saddle past Tipsoo Peak		0.8	1861.4	7300	D4
Maidu Lake Trail 3725A		4.3	1865.7	6190	D5
Crossing of county-line ridge		1.3	1867.0	6490	D7
Descend to a crest saddle		2.3	1869.3	6470	D7
Diagonal northeast to a saddle		1.9	1871.2	6300	D6
Tolo Camp, junction to Six Horse Spring	w: 0.33m E	0.7	1871.9	6190	D6
	Water Alert (↑):	16.2m			
Traverse over to another saddle		0.6	1872.5	6235	D6
Tenas Trail 1445		1.3	1873.8	6610	D8
Spur trail to parking area by old Cascade Lakes Road	R	3.7	1877.5	5845	D8
Windigo Pass, new Cascade Lakes Road 60, water cross country 0.1m E	w,R: 0.10m E	0.3	1877.8	5820	D8
Minor crest saddle to lakelet	w: 0.10m NW	2.3	1880.1	6620	D8
saddle by southwest ridge of Cowhorn Mountain		1.6	1881.7	7100	D8
Stagnant pool	w	3.1	1884.8	6380	D9
Summit Lake's south shore	w	4.1	1888.9	5560	D9
Road 700	R	0.2	1889.1	5570	D9

Oregon

Landmark	Facilities	Diff	S->N	Elev	Map
Road 6010 near Summit Lake Campground	R	1.4	1890.5	5590	D9
Leaving west shore of last unmapped lake	w	1.1	1891.6	5670	D9
South shore of one accessible lake	w	0.9	1892.5	5860	D9
Northwest up a switchback, plenty of ponds north on PCT		2.8	1895.3	6560	D11
North shore of a green, unnamed lake, plenty of ponds south on PCT	w	7.2	1902.5	6030	D11
Descend to an even larger lake	w	0.6	1903.1	5840	D11
Junction to well-hidden Midnight Lake	w: 0.05m E	2.5	1905.6	5370	D13
Pengra Pass		1.5	1907.1	5003	D13
Cascade Summit P.O., OR 97425, (541) 433-2548	PO,w,G,sh,r: 1.40m SE	0.0	1907.1	5003	D13
Old Oregon Skyline Trail		0.5	1907.6	5040	D13
Highway 58 near Willamette Pass	R	1.1	1908.7	5090	D13
Trailhead-parking spur trail		0.2	1908.9	5130	E1
Ridge above South (Lower) Rosary Lake	w	2.0	1910.9	5730	E1
Middle Rosary Lake	w	0.6	1911.5	5830	E1
North Rosary Lake	w	0.3	1911.8	5830	E1
Maiden Lake Trail 41		0.6	1912.4	6060	E1
Switchback west to a saddle		0.5	1912.9	6170	E1
Minor saddle		1.3	1914.2	6070	E2
Maiden Peak Trail 3681		1.2	1915.4	5730	E2
Old OST route		0.6	1916.0	5400	E2
Bobby Lake Trail 3663		1.5	1917.5	5440	E2
Moore Creek Trail 40 to Bobby Lake	w: 0.25m E	0.2	1917.7	5470	E2
Climb northwest to a saddle		1.4	1919.1	5980	E2
Twin Peaks Trail 3595		1.3	1920.4	6220	E3
cluster of three ponds		2.4	1922.8	6320	E3

Oregon

Landmark	Facilities	Diff	S->N	Elev	Map
Charlton Lake Trail 3570	w: 0.10m SE	2.5	1925.3	5725	E3
Road 5897	R	0.6	1925.9	5840	E3
Lily Lake Trail 19	w: 0.75m NE	1.4	1927.3	5965	E3
Taylor Lake	w	3.3	1930.6	5550	E5
Road 600 at Irish Lake	w,R	0.3	1930.9	5549	E5
Riffle Lake	w	0.8	1931.7	5575	E5
Climb to a higher ridge		1.2	1932.9	5730	E5
East shore of Brahma Lake	w	0.6	1933.5	5657	E5
Jezebel Lake	w	1.1	1934.6	5855	E5
Stormy Lake	w	1.0	1935.6	6045	E5
Blaze Lake	w	0.3	1935.9	5950	E5
Cougar Flat		2.1	1938.0	5750	E6
Tadpole Lake	w	2.0	1940.0	5340	E6
Elk Creek and Winopee Lake trails		0.4	1940.4	5250	E6
Snowshoe Lake Trail 33	w	1.2	1941.6	5250	E6
Mink Lake Loop Trail 3526	w	0.4	1942.0	5160	E6
Spur trail to Moody Lake	w: 0.10m N	1.5	1943.5	5040	E6
Cliff Lake Trail, Mink Lake Loop Trail 3526	w	0.8	1944.3	5130	E6
Climb gently to a seasonal creek		0.8	1945.1	5225	E6
Goose Rock and Senoj Lake trails		0.6	1945.7	5330	E6
Large, east-end campsite	w	0.4	1946.1	5320	E6
Island Lake	w	0.5	1946.6	5438	E6
Dumbbell Lake	w	0.7	1947.3	5502	E6
Past many ponds to a low divide		2.2	1949.5	5660	E6
Junction with old OST		0.5	1950.0	5460	E7
Sunset Lake Trail 3517A		1.9	1951.9	5235	E7
Island Meadow Trail to Elk Lake 3/3517		1.3	1953.2	5250	E7
Elk Lake Resort, Century Drive (P.O. Box 789), Bend, OR 97709, (541) 317-2994	w,G,M: 1.10m E	0.0	1953.2	5250	E7
Horse Lake Trail 2/3516		1.3	1954.5	5300	E7

Oregon

Landmark	Facilities	Diff	S->N	Elev	Map
Camelot Lake	w	4.4	1958.9	5980	E9
Sisters Mirror Lake	w	0.1	1959.0	5980	E9
Junction with Nash Lake Trail 3527 and Mirror Lake Trail 20		0.4	1959.4	5990	E9
Junction with Wickiup Plain Trail		0.3	1959.7	6030	E9
Broad county-line divide		1.2	1960.9	6210	E9
Meet Wickiup Plain Trail		0.5	1961.4	6160	E9
Descend to a creek	w	1.2	1962.6	6010	E10
North fork of Mesa Creek	w	0.8	1963.4	5700	E10
Junction with James Creek Trail		0.6	1964.0	5920	E10
Cross Hinton Creek	w	2.1	1966.1	6320	E10
Cross Separation Creek	w	0.5	1966.6	6400	E10
Clear lakelet with good campsites	w	0.4	1967.0	6460	E10
Foley Ridge Trail 3511		1.3	1968.3	6270	E10
Linton Meadows Trail		1.7	1970.0	6440	E10
Obsidian Trail 3528	w	2.1	1972.1	6380	E12
Glacier Way Trail 3528A	w	1.6	1973.7	6370	E12
White Branch creek		0.9	1974.6	6210	E12
Minnie Scott Spring	w	2.2	1976.8	6650	E12
Scott Trail 3551		0.9	1977.7	6300	E12
South Matthieu Lake	w	2.5	1980.2	6040	E12
South junction with old OST route to North Matthieu Lake		0.1	1980.3	6070	E12
North junction with old OST route to North Matthieu Lake		2.1	1982.4	5450	E13
Trail to Lava Camp Lake, junction to a large trailhead parking area	w: 0.25m NE	0.7	1983.1	5310	E13
	Water Alert (↓):	16.5m			
McKenzie Highway (242)	R	1.1	1984.2	5280	E13
Town of Sisters	w,G: 15.00m NE	0.0	1984.2	5280	E13
Highway 242 at McKenzie	R	0.3	1984.5	5210	E13

Oregon

Landmark	Facilities	Diff	S->N	Elev	Map
Pass, small trailhead parking area					
Spur trail to summit of Little Belknap		2.3	1986.8	6120	F1
Fresh looking lava flow		2.5	1989.3	5320	F1
Washington Ponds spur trail, very difficult to find		2.5	1991.8	5710	F1
Coldwater Spring		2.4	1994.2	5200	F1
Unmarked climber's trail to Washington Peak		0.5	1994.7	5050	F2
Descend north to fork with broad trail		0.9	1995.6	4760	F2
Old Santiam Wagon Road	R	2.0	1997.6	4680	F2
Lily-pad pond	w	2.0	1999.6	4790	F2
	Water Alert (↑):	16.8m			
Cross Santiam Highway (US Highway 20), junction to Douthit Spring	w,R: 0.30m E	2.0	2001.6	4810	F3
Santiam Lake Trail 3491		1.4	2003.0	5200	F3
Curve north-northwest, cross-country hike to Summit Lake	w: 0.40m NE	2.5	2005.5	6000	F3
Round the peak's northwest spur		2.6	2008.1	6390	F3
Saddle along the Cascade divide		0.5	2008.6	6500	F3
Minto Pass Trail 3437 south to Wasco Lake	w: 0.25m S	3.2	2011.8	5350	F4
Wasco Lake loop trail (#65)	w: 0.50m SE	0.5	2012.3	5430	F4
Southeast spur of Peak 6488		2.2	2014.5	6210	F4
Rockpile Lake	w	1.0	2015.5	6250	F4
Trail forks as Trail 69		0.5	2016.0	6140	F4
Swallow Lake Trail 3488		1.0	2017.0	6300	F4
Reach a saddle		1.2	2018.2	6400	F5
Unsigned trail to emerald Carl Lake	w: 1.00m SE	0.9	2019.1	6240	F5
Small, grassy meadow, water in pond	w	1.7	2020.8	6240	F5

Oregon

Landmark	Facilities	Diff	S->N	Elev	Map
Escarpment where Mt. Jefferson towers above		0.4	2021.2	6340	F5
Unsigned trail climbs back to divide		0.7	2021.9	6130	F5
Start of Pamelia Lake alternate route, reach a saddle		0.5	2022.4	5910	F5
West shore of placid Shale Lake	w	1.8	2024.2	5910	F5
End of Pamelia Lake alternate route, junction with old OST		4.5	2028.7	4320	F5
Cross Milk Creek	w	0.2	2028.9	4320	F5
Woodpecker Trail 3442		1.6	2030.5	5040	F6
Russell Creek	w	2.8	2033.3	5520	F6
Jefferson Park Trail 3429		0.6	2033.9	5640	F6
Ford Whitewater Creek	w	0.4	2034.3	5680	F6
Spur to Scout Lake		0.5	2034.8	5860	F6
Spur trail to Scout and Bays lakes		0.3	2035.1	5930	F6
Junction with South Breitenbush Trail 3375		0.5	2035.6	5870	F6
Cross South Fork Breitenbush River	w	0.1	2035.7	5840	F6
Viewpoint		2.0	2037.7	6920	F6
Low saddle		2.1	2039.8	6150	F7
Skyline Road 42 (4220) near Breitenbush Lake	w,R	1.6	2041.4	5500	F7
East shore of a shallow lake	w	0.5	2041.9	5750	F7
Junction with old OST route, now Gibson Trail 708		1.0	2042.9	5510	F7
Horseshoe Saddle Trail 712		0.1	2043.0	5520	F7
Ruddy Hill Trail 714		0.3	2043.3	5600	F7
Many Lakes Viewpoint		1.2	2044.5	5660	F7
Upper Lake, very good campsite	w	0.9	2045.4	5380	F7
Cigar Lake	w	0.4	2045.8	5350	F7
Junction to Fork Lake		0.4	2046.2	5280	F7

Oregon

Landmark	Facilities	Diff	S->N	Elev	Map
Small triangular, semiclear lake	w	0.9	2047.1	5180	F7
Head Lake	w	0.7	2047.8	4950	F7
Olallie Lake Ranger Station, c/o Clackamas Ranger District, 595 NW Industrial Way, Estacada, OR 97023	w,G: 0.10m E	0.0	2047.8	4950	F7
Skyline Road 42 (4220) near Olallie Lake Guard Station	R	0.1	2047.9	4990	F7
Olallie Butte Trail 720		2.2	2050.1	4680	F7
Junction with old OST, now known as Lodgepole Trail 706		1.0	2051.1	4570	F8
Russ Lake Trail 716		0.3	2051.4	4550	F8
Jude Lake	w	0.2	2051.6	4600	F8
Lemiti Creek	w	6.0	2057.6	4360	F8
Junction to Trooper Springs	w: 0.05m SW	0.5	2058.1	4400	F8
Chinquapin Viewpoint		2.8	2060.9	5000	F8
Cross a saddle		0.8	2061.7	4980	F9
Spur trail to view north of Mt. Hood		1.4	2063.1	4640	F9
Spur trail to a seeping spring	w: 0.05m W	3.3	2066.4	3860	F9
Cross Warm Springs River	w	2.3	2068.7	3300	F10
Spur trail to a another spring	w: 0.05m SE	0.4	2069.1	3450	F10
Junction with Road 4245	R	1.0	2070.1	3720	F10
East slope of Summit Butte		1.7	2071.8	4230	F10
Unseen Red Wolf Pass		1.4	2073.2	4120	F10
Reach a jeep road	R	0.8	2074.0	3990	F10
Close Road S549	R	1.3	2075.3	3580	F10
Junction with Miller Trail 534 to Clackamas Lake Campground	w: 0.30m NW	1.9	2077.2	3400	F11
Oak Grove Fork Clackamas River		0.7	2077.9	3350	F11
Skyline Road 42	R	0.2	2078.1	3370	F11

Oregon

Landmark	Facilities	Diff	S->N	Elev	Map
Timothy Trail 528		1.4	2079.5	3320	F11
Crater Creek	w	4.3	2083.8	3220	F11
Little Crater Lake Trail 500	w: 0.12m E	0.2	2084.0	3230	F11
Road 5890	R	1.6	2085.6	3360	F11
Abbot Road 58	R	1.4	2087.0	3860	F12
Linney Creek Road 240	R	0.8	2087.8	3880	F12
Pass a small campsite with seeping spring	w	0.2	2088.0	3910	F12
Climb north to a saddle		0.5	2088.5	4010	F12
U.S. Highway 26 at Wapinitia Pass	R	3.5	2092.0	3910	F13
Switchback north to a near-crest junction to Twin Lakes trail		1.2	2093.2	4360	F13
Traverse north to a broad saddle		1.1	2094.3	4450	F14
Reunion with the loop trail		0.5	2094.8	4500	F14
Palmateer View Trail 482		0.5	2095.3	4550	F14
Old section of Highway 35 at Barlow Pass	R	1.5	2096.8	4157	F14
Cross new section of Highway 35 near Barlow Pass	w,R: 0.10m E	0.2	2097.0	4155	F14
Government Camp P.O., 88331 E Government Camp Loop, Government Camp, OR, 97028, (800) 275-8777	PO,w,G: 6.00m W	0.0	2097.0	4155	F14
Gully with a campsite	w	2.7	2099.7	4870	G1
Join the Timberline Trail 600		0.9	2100.6	5340	G1
White River Buried Forest Overlook		0.8	2101.4	5790	G1
Cross upper Salmon River	w	0.3	2101.7	5900	G1
Spur trail to Timberline Lodge		0.2	2101.9	5960	G1
Timberline Lodge		0.1	2102.0	5940	G1
Timberline Ski Area, WY'East Store, Timberline Lodge, OR 97028, (541) 231-7979	w,G,M,L,r: 0.10m S	0.0	2102.0	5940	G1
Past a microwave tower		0.2	2102.2	5980	G1

Oregon

Landmark	Facilities	Diff	S->N	Elev	Map
Cross Little Zigzag creek	w	0.9	2103.1	5760	G1
Hidden Lake Trail 779		0.4	2103.5	5680	G1
Cross silty Zigzag River	w	1.3	2104.8	4890	G1
PCT splits to two routes		0.5	2105.3	5140	G1
Meet Paradise Park Trail 778		1.0	2106.3	5740	G1
Lost Creek	w	0.2	2106.5	5720	G1
Paradise Park Shelter	w	0.1	2106.6	5730	G1
Meet PCT horse trail		1.1	2107.7	5400	G2
Scout Camp after Sandy River	w	3.0	2110.7	3400	G2
Flat bench, suitable for camping	w	0.3	2111.0	3270	G3
Ramona Falls Loop Trail 797		0.1	2111.1	3320	G3
Ramona Falls	w	0.4	2111.5	3460	G3
Yocum Ridge Trail 771		0.6	2112.1	4000	G3
Cluster of small campsites	w	2.0	2114.1	4100	G3
Spur trail to a campsite	w	0.4	2114.5	4060	G3
Junction with the old OST, leave the Timberline Trail		2.3	2116.8	4270	G3
Crest's end		1.4	2118.2	4200	G3
Lolo Pass Road 18 at Lolo Pass	R	1.4	2119.6	3420	G4
Trickling creek	w	0.4	2120.0	3520	G4
Junction with Huckleberry Mountain Trail 617 to Salvation Spring Camp	w: 0.30m N	3.9	2123.9	4020	G4
Preachers/Devils saddle		0.9	2124.8	4340	G4
Descend west to a notch		1.9	2126.7	4250	G4
Buck Peak Trail 615		0.5	2127.2	4500	G4
Discover a small spring	w	0.4	2127.6	4340	G4
Reach the ridge again		0.3	2127.9	4230	G5
Reach abandoned OST		2.2	2130.1	4190	G5
Larch Mountain Road 2030	R	0.1	2130.2	4240	G5
Spur of Indian Mountain with view of Mts. St. Helens, Rainier, Adams		1.6	2131.8	4400	G5
Indian Springs Campground	w	0.3	2132.1	4300	G5
Junction with Eagle Creek Trail 440 to Wahtum Lake	w	2.6	2134.7	3750	G5

Oregon

Landmark	Facilities	Diff	S->N	Elev	Map
Lateral trail to Wahtum Lake Campground		0.2	2134.9	3750	G5
Chinidere Mountain Trail		1.8	2136.7	4270	G5
Saddle to a viewpoint		0.6	2137.3	4140	G5
Second saddle		1.4	2138.7	3830	G6
Camp Smokey saddle, third saddle	w: 0.12m W	0.8	2139.5	3810	G6
Benson Way Trail 405B		0.5	2140.0	4100	G6
Ruckel Creek Trail 405	w: 0.50m W	0.9	2140.9	4110	G7
Benson Ruckel Trail		0.7	2141.6	3980	G7
Second Benson Way Trail 405B		0.7	2142.3	3760	G7
Another waterless campsite		0.6	2142.9	3680	G7
Teakettle Spring	w	0.3	2143.2	3360	G7
Junction to Columbia Gorge Work Center, lateral trail to Herman Creek		3.0	2146.2	1120	G7
Cross a creek	w	0.5	2146.7	960	G7
Misnamed Dry Creek, camping possible	w	1.8	2148.5	720	G7
Power-line road	R	0.7	2149.2	680	G7
SE Undine Street		1.0	2150.2	240	G7
Cascade Locks P.O., OR 97014, (541) 374-8410	PO,w,G,M,L,sh, r: 0.25m NE	0.0	2150.2	240	G7
Bridge of the Gods, east end		0.1	2150.3	200	G7

Washington

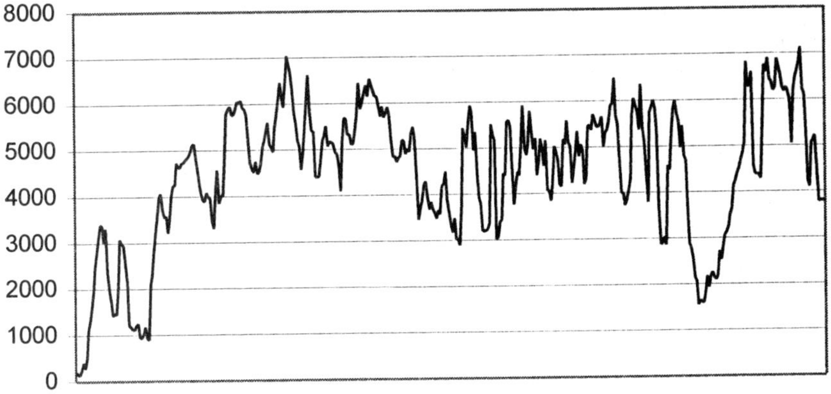

Section Total Mileage: 508.4 miles

Landmark	Facilities	Diff	S->N	Elev	Map
Bridge of the Gods, west end		0.5	2150.8	200	H1
PCT trailhead		0.2	2151.0	150	H1
Cross a paved road	R	0.8	2151.8	140	H1
Climb to a ridge, meet Tamehnous Trail 25		0.4	2152.2	250	H1
Reach a utility road	R	2.1	2154.3	410	H1
Junction to Gillette Lake	w: 0.10m E	0.3	2154.6	280	H1
Bridge across Greenleaf Creek	w	0.9	2155.5	510	H2
Low ridgecrest		1.9	2157.4	1100	H2
Cross a road	R	0.6	2158.0	1300	H2
Recross road	w,R: 0.20m N	0.3	2158.3	1600	H2
	Water Alert (↓):	12.8m			
Southwest up to a larger ridge		0.9	2159.2	1970	H2
Viewpoint, spring near Table Mountain		1.3	2160.5	2480	H2
Nearby road	R	0.8	2161.3	2790	H2
Ridge above a powerline		0.5	2161.8	3120	H2

Landmark	Facilities	Diff	S->N	Elev	Map
saddle					
Climb to a saddle and cross it, first view of Three Corner Rock		0.7	2162.5	3400	H2
Come to a seep, maybe dry		0.3	2162.8	3370	H2
Crestline road	R	1.3	2164.1	3020	H2
Spur trail to Three Corner Rock water trough, has a leak		2.0	2166.1	3320	H3
Viewless saddle by Road 2090	R	1.9	2168.0	2360	H3
Crest gap		0.5	2168.5	1980	H4
Road 2000	R	1.8	2170.3	1720	H4
Rock Creek	w	0.8	2171.1	1420	H4
	Water Alert (↑):	13.0m			
Snag Creek	w	0.4	2171.5	1470	H4
Road 2070	w,R: 0.12m SE	0.3	2171.8	1450	H4
Seasonal creeklet	w	1.8	2173.6	2080	H4
South-trending ridge		1.8	2175.4	3080	H4
Second saddle, almost touch Road 41	R	0.7	2176.1	2985	H4
Cross Sunset-Hemlock Road 41	R	0.8	2176.9	2950	H4
Forest to main ridge		1.0	2177.9	2550	H4
Northeast down to a viewless saddle		0.7	2178.6	2150	H4
Cross a wide, splashing tributary of Trout Creek	w	2.0	2180.6	1210	H4
Cross Road 43 alongside Trout creek	R	0.3	2180.9	1180	H5
Southeast to Road 417	R	0.8	2181.7	1120	H5
Junction to Wind River Ranger Station		0.1	2181.8	1120	H5
Bunker Hill Trail		0.5	2182.3	1210	H5
Cross a crest		0.7	2183.0	1250	H5
Little Soda Springs Road 54	R	0.8	2183.8	940	H5
Cross Wind River	w	0.3	2184.1	940	H5
Wind River Road	R	0.2	2184.3	1020	H5
Cross Road 6517	R	0.8	2185.1	1180	H5
Down to Panther Creek Road 65	R	1.2	2186.3	930	H5

Washington

Landmark	Facilities	Diff	S->N	Elev	Map
Panther Creek	w	0.2	2186.5	900	H5
Westernmost end of a ridge		2.1	2188.6	2100	H6
Saddle where a good dirt road starts	R	1.1	2189.7	2300	H6
Junction with Road 68	R	1.3	2191.0	2810	H6
Descend to a broad, open saddle		1.7	2192.7	3214	H6
Junction to Cedar Creek, about 350 feet drop	w: 0.25m S	1.2	2193.9	3580	H7
Junction with the old Cascade Crest Trail		1.0	2194.9	4000	H7
Junction with the Big Huckleberry Mountain summit trail		0.1	2195.0	4070	H7
Second saddle		1.2	2196.2	3730	H7
Descend to a gully which has a reliable spring	w	0.5	2196.7	3550	H7
Reach a viewless, broad saddle		0.8	2197.5	3580	H7
Head towards Road 6801	R	0.8	2198.3	3220	H7
Road 60, back of Crest Campground	R	3.5	2201.8	3490	H8
Duck pond named as Sheep Lake	w	1.9	2203.7	4020	H8
Green Lake	w	1.1	2204.8	4250	H8
Junction with Shortcut Trail 171A		0.4	2205.2	4240	H8
Switchback to a saddle		2.9	2208.1	4730	H8
Outlet creek of Lake Sebago	w	0.9	2209.0	4640	H8
Blue Lake	w	0.2	2209.2	4630	H8
Junction with East Crater Trail 48	w	1.9	2211.1	4730	H9
Meet Lemei Lake Trail 33A	w	0.1	2211.2	4730	H9
Bear Lake, Elk Lake Trail 176	w	1.0	2212.2	4790	H9
Slope above east end of Deer Lake	w	0.4	2212.6	4830	H9
Indian Heaven Trail 33		0.1	2212.7	4880	H9
Placid Lake Trail 29		1.1	2213.8	4980	H9
Second saddle to a campsite		0.5	2214.3	5110	H9

Washington

Landmark	Facilities	Diff	S->N	Elev	Map
West end of Cultus Creek Trail 108		0.4	2214.7	5150	H9
Crest saddle		1.2	2215.9	4850	H9
Summit's footpath		1.4	2217.3	4570	H9
Cross Road 24	R	1.2	2218.5	4260	H9
Descend to a saddle		1.4	2219.9	4070	H10
Road 8851	R	2.5	2222.4	3915	H10
Outlet of Big Mosquito Lake	w	0.1	2222.5	3900	H10
Cross a dirt road	R	2.4	2224.9	4090	H10
Steamboat Lake spur trail	w	0.4	2225.3	3980	H10
End of the alternate trail, climbs to Steamboat Lake Campground		0.8	2226.1	3970	H11
Junction with Road 88	R	1.2	2227.3	3470	H11
Trout Lake Creek	w	0.4	2227.7	3310	H11
Road 8810	R	2.1	2229.8	4140	H12
Reach the crest		0.6	2230.4	4570	H12
Road 23, trailhead at Road 8810	w,R	2.7	2233.1	3854	H12
Road 521	R	0.9	2234.0	4020	H12
Swampy Creek	w	0.3	2234.3	4020	H12
Spring, 100 yards past White Salmon River	w	2.4	2236.7	4900	H12
Junction with Stagman Ridge Trail 12		2.5	2239.2	5790	H13
Junction with Round the Mountain Trail 9		0.5	2239.7	5900	H13
Traverse to a saddle, east of Burnt Rock		3.2	2242.9	5950	H13
Sheep Lake	w	0.3	2243.2	5768	H13
Cross Riley Creek	w	0.2	2243.4	5770	H13
Mutton Creek	w	1.3	2244.7	5900	H13
Cross Lewis River	w	1.3	2246.0	6060	H13
Junction with Divide Camp Trail 112	w	0.3	2246.3	6020	H13
Junction with Killen Creek Trail 113	w	1.4	2247.7	6084	H14
Cross Killen Creek	w	0.8	2248.5	5920	H14

Washington

Landmark	Facilities	Diff	S->N	Elev	Map
Highline Trail 114		0.2	2248.7	5900	H14
Readily accessible second pond, first one better	w	0.4	2249.1	5772	H14
Trail to junction with Highline Trail		2.0	2251.1	5231	H14
Cross Muddy Fork	w	1.6	2252.7	4740	H14
Westward to a very good campsite	w	0.5	2253.2	4590	H14
Trailside Lava Spring	w	0.3	2253.5	4520	H14
Road 5603	R	1.6	2255.1	4750	H14
East-west road near Midway site, junction with Road 115	R	2.0	2257.1	4490	H15
Closed Road 655	R	0.1	2257.2	4520	H15
Cross Midway Creek	w	0.4	2257.6	4690	H15
Leave last pond	w	2.8	2260.4	5070	H15
Climb to a switchback		1.6	2262.0	5220	H15
Climb to a saddle, pass two small ponds		0.7	2262.7	5450	H15
Prominent ridgecrest		0.8	2263.5	5600	H16
Cross a trickling creek	w	1.4	2264.9	5140	H16
50-yard pond	w	0.5	2265.4	5050	H16
Walupt Lake Trail 101		3.4	2268.8	4960	H17
Walupt Creek	w	3.9	2272.7	5480	H17
Sheep Lake near Nannie Ridge Trail 98	w	0.6	2273.3	5760	H17
Crest saddle		1.4	2274.7	6100	H17
Cispus Pass		0.9	2275.6	6460	H17
Campsite beside easternmost tributary of Cispus River	w	0.6	2276.2	6130	H17
Junction with Trail 86 to Bypass Camp	w: 0.60m W	1.6	2277.8	5930	H17
Trail 96 junction		1.0	2278.8	6420	H17
Dana May Yelverton Shelter, may not be safe, broken		1.1	2279.9	7040	H18
Down to crest saddle		1.0	2280.9	6850	H18
Upper end of Coyote Trail 79		1.3	2282.2	6680	H18
Bleak, alpine campsites	w	0.3	2282.5	6320	H18

Washington

Landmark	Facilities	Diff	S->N	Elev	Map
Saddle, former Cascade Crest Trail drops southeast		1.3	2283.8	5820	H18
Almost touches a crest saddle		0.6	2284.4	5580	H18
Junction with the old CCT		0.5	2284.9	5200	H18
Saddle that holds Lutz Lake and small campsites	w	0.6	2285.5	5100	H18
Tieton Pass		1.0	2286.5	4570	H19
Cross east over the divide		1.5	2288.0	4930	H19
Junction with Trail 1117 to Hidden Spring	w: 0.30m E	1.8	2289.8	5520	H19
West on a mid 80's segment		0.9	2290.7	6040	H19
Top a narrow ridge		1.2	2291.9	6620	H19
Junction with Chairlift Trail		2.5	2294.4	5830	H19
Junction with Hogback Trail 1144		1.2	2295.6	5400	H19
Ginnette Lake	w	0.2	2295.8	5400	H19
U.S. Highway 12 (old state Highway 14) near White Pass	R	2.2	2298.0	4405	H19
White Pass Rural Branch P.O., (At the Kracker Barrel Store), 48851 US Highway 12, Naches, WA 98937, (425) 672-3105	PO,w,G,M,sh,r, R: 0.70m W	0.0	2298.0	4405	H19
Start from the parking lot		0.2	2298.2	4415	I1
Junction with Dark Meadows Trail 1107	w	1.1	2299.3	4780	I1
Deer Lake	w	1.0	2300.3	5206	I1
Sand Lake	w	0.5	2300.8	5295	I1
Cortright Creek Trail 57		2.0	2302.8	5520	I1
Buesch Lake	w	1.1	2303.9	5081	I1
Good picnic spot next to a slender lake	w	1.1	2305.0	5180	I1
Cowlitz Pass		0.5	2305.5	5160	I1
Cowlitz Trail 44		0.2	2305.7	5140	I1
Snow Lake		2.1	2307.8	4935	I2
Pothole Trail 45		0.8	2308.6	4900	I2
Packer campsite	w	2.9	2311.5	4620	I2
Bumping River ford by	w	1.1	2312.6	4100	I3

Landmark	Facilities	Diff	S->N	Elev	Map
Bumping Lake Trail, Fish Lake					
Reliable drinkable rill	w	2.7	2315.3	5170	I3
Laughingwater Trail 22		1.6	2316.9	5690	I3
Trail 380 to Two Lakes	w: 0.30m SE	1.6	2318.5	5660	I3
American Ridge Trail 958		2.6	2321.1	5320	I4
Anderson Lake	w	1.4	2322.5	5340	I4
Dewey Lake	w	1.8	2324.3	5112	I4
Dewey Lake Trail 968	w	0.5	2324.8	5130	I4
Highway 410 at Chinook Pass	w,R: 0.33m S	2.7	2327.5	5432	I5
Sheep Lake	w	2.2	2329.7	5750	I5
Sourdough Gap		1.2	2330.9	6440	I6
Meet Silver Creek Trail 1192		2.1	2333.0	5882	I6
Obscure trail signed FOG CITY and GOLD HILL		1.1	2334.1	6040	I6
Meet two trails, to Gold Hill and to Union Creek Trail 956		0.3	2334.4	6200	I6
Blue Bell Pass		0.4	2334.8	6390	I6
Bullion Basin Trail 1156		0.9	2335.7	6150	I6
Scout Pass		1.5	2337.2	6530	I6
Junction to Basin Lake, excellent camping	w: 0.50m SE	0.6	2337.8	6390	I6
Big Crow Basin Spring near Norse Peak Trail, reliable spring	w	0.4	2338.2	6290	I6
Barnard Saddle		0.8	2339.0	6150	I7
Hayden Pass		0.3	2339.3	6150	I7
Sign LITTLE CROW BASIN	w: 0.10m S	0.4	2339.7	5930	I7
Martinson Gap		1.4	2341.1	5720	I7
Arch Rock Way 1187		2.1	2343.2	5930	I8
Unsigned spoor to Morgan Springs	w: 0.25m E	0.5	2343.7	5700	I8
Cougar Valley Trail		0.3	2344.0	5780	I9
Junction to summit		0.5	2344.5	5920	I9
Spur trail to Arch Rock shelter	w: 0.10m W	0.8	2345.3	5760	I9
Louisiana Saddle		1.5	2346.8	5220	I9

Washington

Landmark	Facilities	Diff	S->N	Elev	Map
Rods Gap		1.1	2347.9	4820	I9
Maggie Way Trail 1186		1.6	2349.5	4850	I9
Camp Urich at Government Meadow	w	0.8	2350.3	4720	I10
Cross historic road	R	0.2	2350.5	4800	I10
Road bends southwest	R	1.1	2351.6	4840	I10
Windy Gap		1.4	2353.0	5200	I10
Spring with two small campsites	w	2.1	2355.1	5180	I10
	Water Alert (↓):	14.4m			
Dirt road that follows the divide fork	R	2.4	2357.5	4890	I11
Cross ridgetop road	R	1.1	2358.6	5000	I11
Green Pass		0.5	2359.1	4940	I11
West Fork Bear Creek Trail		1.0	2360.1	5340	I11
Granite Creek Trail 1326 on Blowout Mountain		1.0	2361.1	5480	I11
Blowout Mountain Trail 1318		1.1	2362.2	5260	I11
Cross two roads to a major saddle	R	2.8	2365.0	4400	I12
Tacoma Pass		2.7	2367.7	3460	I12
Sheets Pass		1.4	2369.1	3720	I12
Seasonal creek	w	0.4	2369.5	3860	I12
	Water Alert (↑):	14.4m			
Broad saddle littered with blowdowns		3.8	2373.3	4200	I12
Low point of the pass		2.3	2375.6	4290	I13
Cross weather station access road	w,R: 0.10m W	1.8	2377.4	3950	I13
Stampede Pass Road 54, junction to Lizard Lake	w,R: 0.20m S	1.0	2378.4	3680	I13
Trail follows to a hairpin on a road	R	2.1	2380.5	3840	I14
Dandy Pass		0.3	2380.8	3680	I14
Come to a creek	w	1.9	2382.7	3600	I14
Stirrup Creek	w	0.8	2383.5	3480	I14
Headwaters of Meadow Creek		2.1	2385.6	3660	I14
West shore of Twilight Lake	w	1.4	2387.0	3575	I14

Washington

Landmark	Facilities	Diff	S->N	Elev	Map
Mirror Lake	w	0.9	2387.9	4195	I15
Mirror Lake Trail 1302		0.4	2388.3	4220	I15
Drop north from sign COLD CREEK TRAIL		0.5	2388.8	4500	I15
Descend to a perennial creek	w: 0.05m W	2.5	2391.3	3900	I15
Olallie Creek	w	0.8	2392.1	3620	I15
Powerline access road	R	0.7	2392.8	3350	I15
Lodge Lake	w	2.0	2394.8	3180	I15
Beaver Lake	w	0.8	2395.6	3480	I15
Interstate 90 at Snoqualmie Pass		1.0	2396.6	3030	I15
P.O. (At the Time Wise Grocery & Deli), 771 State Route 906, Snoqualmie Pass, WA 98068, (206) 434-6141	PO,w,G,M,L,r: 0.30m SE	0.0	2396.6	3030	I15
Northbound Trailhead across I-90		0.5	2397.1	2900	J1
Red Mountain trail 1033	w: 0.30m N	2.7	2399.8	3820	J1
Cross east side of the crest		3.2	2403.0	5440	J1
Crest saddle between Ridge and Gravel lakes	w	1.1	2404.1	5270	J1
Forested saddle between Joe and Edds lakes		2.2	2406.3	5030	J1
Huckleberry Saddle		1.5	2407.8	5560	J2
Needle Sight Gap		0.6	2408.4	5930	J2
Chikamin Pass		2.5	2410.9	5780	J2
Spur to more campsites near Park Lakes	w	1.4	2412.3	4960	J2
Spur of Three Queens		0.8	2413.1	5350	J2
Spectacle Lake Trail 1306		1.6	2414.7	4440	J2
Delate Creek, has a campsite	w	1.2	2415.9	3920	J2
Small campsite	w	0.3	2416.2	3800	J2
Pete Lake Trail 1323		1.8	2418.0	3210	J2
Lemah Creek	w	0.8	2418.8	3200	J2
Lemah Meadow Trail 1323B	w	0.7	2419.5	3210	J2
A couple of campsites	w	0.1	2419.6	3240	J2
Switchback out of Lemah Creek	w: 0.25m NW	0.7	2420.3	3370	J2

Landmark	Facilities	Diff	S->N	Elev	Map
Secluded cirque with a chilly tarn	w	5.3	2425.6	5520	J3
Cross the inlet	w	1.3	2426.9	5300	J4
Waptus Burn Trail 1329C		1.7	2428.6	5180	J3
Waptus River	w	4.8	2433.4	3020	J4
Waptus River Trail 1310	w	0.8	2434.2	3070	J4
Second stream with campsite near Spade Lake Trail 1337	w	1.5	2435.7	3400	J4
Spinola Creek Trail 1310A		1.1	2436.8	3440	J5
Lake Vicente Trail 1365		3.8	2440.6	4440	J6
Deep Lake's campsite access trail	w	0.5	2441.1	4400	J6
Trail 1375		3.0	2444.1	5560	J6
Cathedral Pass		0.2	2444.3	5610	J6
Few small tarns		0.1	2444.4	5460	J6
Junction of two streams	w	2.0	2446.4	4600	J6
Cross second creek carefully, drains Mt. Daniel's NE slopes	w	1.4	2447.8	3770	J6
Cross headwaters of Cle Elum drainage where trail turns East	w	1.0	2448.8	4180	J6
Deception Pass		0.8	2449.6	4470	J6
Cross a stream near a campsite	w	1.9	2451.5	4400	J6
Cross outlet of Deception Lakes	w	1.5	2453.0	5040	J7
Pieper Pass		2.0	2455.0	5920	J7
Glacier Lake campsite, past a campsite	w	2.0	2457.0	5000	J7
Surprise Lake Trail 1060	w	0.8	2457.8	4840	J7
Trap Pass Trail 1060A		1.0	2458.8	5080	J7
Trap Pass		0.9	2459.7	5800	J7
Access trail to Trap Lake		0.8	2460.5	5350	J8
Campsite beside a seasonal creek	w	1.2	2461.7	4970	J8
Climb to a notch		0.7	2462.4	5210	J8
Hope Lake	w	1.1	2463.5	4400	J8

Washington

Landmark	Facilities	Diff	S->N	Elev	Map
North end of Mig Lake	w	0.7	2464.2	4670	J8
Unnamed crest saddle		1.8	2466.0	5190	J8
Josephine Lake's cirque		0.8	2466.8	4980	J8
North shore of Lake Susan Jane	w	0.5	2467.3	4600	J8
Saddle near the top of a chairlift		2.2	2469.5	5160	J8
Highway 2 at Stevens Pass, parking area	R	2.1	2471.6	4060	J8
Skykomish P.O., WA 98288, (360) 677-2241	PO,w,G,M,L,r: 14.00m W	0.0	2471.6	4060	J8
3-yard wide tributary of Nason Creek	w	2.5	2474.1	3850	K1
Meadow where Nason Creek flows	w	1.0	2475.1	4220	K1
Switchback up to a saddle		1.7	2476.8	5030	K1
Spur trail to Lake Valhalla	w	0.3	2477.1	4900	K1
Smithbrook Trail 1590		1.8	2478.9	4700	K1
Delightful cascade	w	1.8	2480.7	4200	K2
Lake Janus	w	0.4	2481.1	4150	K2
Reach a crest		1.6	2482.7	5180	K2
Meadow with faint trail to Glasses Lake		0.8	2483.5	5070	K3
West shoulder of Grizzly Peak		2.1	2485.6	5580	K3
Cross the crest above Grizzly Lake		1.4	2487.0	5120	K3
Shadeless campsite		0.2	2487.2	5030	K3
Wenatchee Pass		1.0	2488.2	4230	K3
Junction with Top Lake Trail 1506		0.6	2488.8	4570	K4
Trail 1057 to Pear Lake's cirque	w	0.7	2489.5	4880	K4
Up to the crest		1.6	2491.1	5350	K4
Fairly reliable creeks	w	2.4	2493.5	4800	K4
Saddle Gap		0.7	2494.2	5060	K4
Junction with West Cady Ridge Trail 1054		0.3	2494.5	4930	K4
Pass Creek Trail 1053, next	w	1.0	2495.5	4200	K4

Landmark	Facilities	Diff	S->N	Elev	Map
to 10-foot wide Pass Creek					
Cady Pass		0.4	2495.9	4310	K4
Switchback to a crest		1.9	2497.8	5470	K4
Lake Sally Ann	w	1.7	2499.5	5479	K5
Junction with Cady Ridge Trail 1532		0.4	2499.9	5380	K5
Wards Pass		0.7	2500.6	5710	K5
Bald Eagle Trail 650		0.6	2501.2	5600	K5
Ridgecrest campsite		0.5	2501.7	5450	K5
Junction with Little Wenatchee River Trail 1525		0.3	2502.0	5440	K5
Spur trail to Trail 1525		0.2	2502.2	5500	K5
Kodak Peak's east ridge		0.7	2502.9	5660	K5
Indian Pass		1.3	2504.2	5020	K5
Murky Kid Pond	w	1.0	2505.2	5320	K6
Lower White Pass		0.7	2505.9	5378	K6
Semi-clear Reflection Pond	w	0.3	2506.2	5560	K6
Junction at White Pass		1.9	2508.1	5904	K7
North Fork Sauk Trail 649		0.6	2508.7	5950	K7
Red Pass		1.3	2510.0	6500	K7
Descend to a lone, three-foot-high cairn		1.4	2511.4	5700	K7
Campsite at a saddle		0.3	2511.7	5500	K7
Last crossing of a swelling creek	w	1.5	2513.2	4700	K7
Cross White Chuck River	w	1.0	2514.2	4000	K7
Baekos Creek	w	1.0	2515.2	3990	K7
Chetwok Creek	w	1.3	2516.5	3730	K7
Sitkum Creek, excellent campsite with pit toilet	w	0.8	2517.3	3852	K8
Kennedy Creek	w	1.2	2518.5	4050	K8
Junction with Kennedy Ridge Trail 643A		0.4	2518.9	4300	K8
Glacier Creek, excellent campsite	w	1.9	2520.8	5640	K8
Junction with Glacier Ridge Trail 658		0.7	2521.5	6050	K8
Cross Pumice Creek	w	0.5	2522.0	5900	K8

Landmark	Facilities	Diff	S->N	Elev	Map
Contour over to a ridge		1.6	2523.6	5770	K8
Cross Fire Creek	w	0.8	2524.4	5370	K8
Fire Creek Pass		1.7	2526.1	6350	K8
Outlet of Mica Lake	w	1.1	2527.2	5430	K8
Open campsite by a small bench, next to Mica Creek	w	0.5	2527.7	5110	K8
Good campsite	w	1.1	2528.8	4400	K8
Milk Creek Trail 790 by Milk Creek	w	1.3	2530.1	3800	K8
Reach a ridgecrest, campsite		2.5	2532.6	5750	K9
Small knoll		1.5	2534.1	5860	K9
Another ridge		0.6	2534.7	6010	K9
Dolly Vista campsite	w	0.7	2535.4	5830	K9
Saddle on Vista Ridge		0.5	2535.9	5380	K9
Signed campsite beside Vista Creek	w	2.6	2538.5	3650	K10
Vista Creek	w	2.1	2540.6	2877	K10
Cross Gamma Creek	w	0.8	2541.4	2910	K10
Junction with Suiattle River Trail 798		0.7	2542.1	3028	K10
Suiattle River access trail	w	0.8	2542.9	2860	K10
Buck Creek Pass trail		4.4	2547.3	4580	K11
Miners Creek	w	0.5	2547.8	4490	K11
Junction with old PCT route		1.5	2549.3	5280	K11
Spur trail to two-tent site		0.7	2550.0	5790	K11
Reach Suiattle Pass with abandoned trail that goes east		0.3	2550.3	5990	K11
Down to a creeklet	w	0.3	2550.6	5730	K11
Junction with Railroad Creek Trail		0.2	2550.8	5550	K11
First downhill to a canyon	w	1.3	2552.1	4980	K11
Spur trail to a one-tent site	w	1.4	2553.5	5450	K11
Spur trail to a two-tent site	w	1.6	2555.1	4810	K11
Spur trail to some tent sites	w	0.2	2555.3	4680	K11
Hemlock Camp	w	2.0	2557.3	3560	K12
Spruce Creek Camp	w	2.7	2560.0	2900	K12
Swamp Creek Camp	w	1.3	2561.3	2780	K12

Washington

Landmark	Facilities	Diff	S->N	Elev	Map
South Fork Agnes Creek	w	1.6	2562.9	2570	K12
Junction with West Fork Agnes Creek Trail 1272, Five Mile Camp	w	1.4	2564.3	2160	K12
Seasonal Trapper Creek	w	1.2	2565.5	2070	K13
Agnes Creek	w	3.6	2569.1	1550	K14
Stehekin River Road	R	0.2	2569.3	1650	K14
High Bridge Ranger Station		0.1	2569.4	1600	K14
Stehekin P.O., WA 98852	PO,w,G,M,L,sh, r: 10.60m E	0.0	2569.4	1600	K14
Junction to Cascade Corral		0.4	2569.8	1860	K14
Coon Lake	w	0.7	2570.5	2180	K14
Junction with Old Wagon Trail		0.8	2571.3	1940	K14
McGregor Creek	w	0.6	2571.9	2195	K14
Buzzard Creek	w	0.4	2572.3	2260	K14
Canim Creek	w	0.7	2573.0	2160	K14
Bridge Creek Ranger Station	w	1.3	2574.3	2105	K14
PCT Bridge Creek trailhead on Stehekin River road	R	0.3	2574.6	2180	K14
Cross Berry Creek	w	1.7	2576.3	2720	K14
Bridge Creek	w	1.0	2577.3	2540	K14
Junction with North Fork Bridge Creek Trail 1233		0.3	2577.6	2810	K14
Maple Creek	w	1.5	2579.1	3070	K14
Spur trail to Six Mile Camp	w: 0.13m SE	1.7	2580.8	3130	K14
Rainbow Lake Trail		0.7	2581.5	3240	K15
Spur trail to the loveliest Bridge Creek campsite: Hide-Away Camp	w: 0.10m SW	1.5	2583.0	3510	K15
Junction with Twisp Pass Trail 1277	w	0.9	2583.9	3635	K15
Ford of Bridge Creek	w	2.2	2586.1	4145	K15
Stiletto Peak Trail 1232		0.2	2586.3	4250	K15
Washington Pass Trail 1275		0.5	2586.8	4420	K16
Spur trail to a parking lot		0.5	2587.3	4510	K16
Outlet creek of Rainy Lake	w	0.7	2588.0	4705	K16
Cross Highway 20's Rainy Pass	R	1.1	2589.1	4855	K16
Porcupine Creek	w	1.5	2590.6	5080	L1

Washington

Landmark	Facilities	Diff	S->N	Elev	Map
Cutthroat Pass		3.6	2594.2	6820	L1
Granite Pass		2.4	2596.6	6290	L1
Large campsite	w	2.2	2598.8	6300	L2
Methow Pass		0.9	2599.7	6600	L2
Golden Creek and Willis Camp	w	4.2	2603.9	4570	L2
West Fork Methow River	w	0.7	2604.6	4390	L3
Merge with old Cascade Crest Trail (now Trail 756)		0.8	2605.4	4380	L3
Junction with Mill Creek Trail 755		0.2	2605.6	4380	L3
West Fork Methow Trail 480, next to Brush Creek	w	1.9	2607.5	4280	L3
Glacier Pass		2.8	2610.3	5520	L3
Alpine-garden pass above South Fork Trout Creek		2.6	2612.9	6750	L4
Pleasant trailside campsite with water	w	1.0	2613.9	6600	L4
Windy, viewful pass on southwest shoulder of Tatie Peak		0.9	2614.8	6900	L4
20 yards before Road 500	R	2.8	2617.6	6440	L4
Minor gap		0.7	2618.3	6390	L4
Harts Pass		1.3	2619.6	6198	L4
Creeklet	w	0.3	2619.9	6260	L4
Junction with a spur trail to a Forest Service road	R	1.1	2621.0	6880	L4
Pass above Benson Creek Camp		2.2	2623.2	6700	L5
Buffalo Pass		0.7	2623.9	6550	L5
Windy Pass		0.9	2624.8	6257	L5
Foggy Pass		2.2	2627.0	6180	L5
Jim Pass		0.7	2627.7	6270	L5
Devils Backbone		1.3	2629.0	6180	L6
Headwaters of Shaw Creek	w	0.6	2629.6	5980	L6
Holman Pass		3.8	2633.4	5050	L6
Spring and a good campsite	w	2.4	2635.8	6200	L6
Canyon Creek to Rock Pass		1.2	2637.0	6491	L6
Misnamed Woody Pass		2.8	2639.8	6624	L7
Faint trail to Mountain Home		2.5	2642.3	6800	L7

Landmark	Facilities	Diff	S->N	Elev	Map
Camp					
Unnamed summit on Lakeview Ridge		0.7	2643.0	7126	L7
Spur trail to Hopkins Lake, campsites	w	1.7	2644.7	6220	L7
Hopkins Pass		0.2	2644.9	6122	L7
Castle Pass	w: 0.75m E	2.5	2647.4	5451	L8
Monument 78, United States-Canada border, close to Castle Creek		4.1	2651.5	4240	L9
Castle Creek	w	0.2	2651.7	4100	L9
Southwest base of Windy Joe Mountain		3.5	2655.2	5070	L9
Junction with the Mt. Frosty Trail	w	0.1	2655.3	5120	L9
Closed Windy Joe fire access road	R	0.7	2656.0	5220	L9
Last crossing of a creek	w	1.2	2657.2	4500	L9
Cross a smaller branch of Similkameen River	w	1.1	2658.3	3780	L9
Beaver Pond parking lot		0.4	2658.7	3800	L9
Manning Park Headquarters, BC, CANADA V0X 1R0	w,r: 0.70m W	0.0	2658.7	3800	L9
Manning Park Lodge, (604) 840-8836	w,G,M,L: 0.90m W	0.0	2658.7	3800	L9

Calendars

January 2000

S	M	T	W	T	F	S
						1
2	3	4	5	6	7	8
9	10	11	12	13	14	15
16	17	18	19	20	21	22
23	24	25	26	27	28	29
30	31					

February 2000

S	M	T	W	T	F	S
		1	2	3	4	5
6	7	8	9	10	11	12
13	14	15	16	17	18	19
20	21	22	23	24	25	26
27	28	29				

March 2000

S	M	T	W	T	F	S
			1	2	3	4
5	6	7	8	9	10	11
12	13	14	15	16	17	18
19	20	21	22	23	24	25
26	27	28	29	30	31	

April 2000

S	M	T	W	T	F	S
						1
2	3	4	5	6	7	8
9	10	11	12	13	14	15
16	17	18	19	20	21	22
23	24	25	26	27	28	29
30						

May 2000

S	M	T	W	T	F	S
	1	2	3	4	5	6
7	8	9	10	11	12	13
14	15	16	17	18	19	20
21	22	23	24	25	26	27
28	29	30	31			

June 2000

S	M	T	W	T	F	S
				1	2	3
4	5	6	7	8	9	10
11	12	13	14	15	16	17
18	19	20	21	22	23	24
25	26	27	28	29	30	

July 2000

S	M	T	W	T	F	S
						1
2	3	4	5	6	7	8
9	10	11	12	13	14	15
16	17	18	19	20	21	22
23	24	25	26	27	28	29
30	31					

August 2000

S	M	T	W	T	F	S
		1	2	3	4	5
6	7	8	9	10	11	12
13	14	15	16	17	18	19
20	21	22	23	24	25	26
27	28	29	30	31		

September 2000

S	M	T	W	T	F	S
					1	2
3	4	5	6	7	8	9
10	11	12	13	14	15	16
17	18	19	20	21	22	23
24	25	26	27	28	29	30

October 2000

S	M	T	W	T	F	S
1	2	3	4	5	6	7
8	9	10	11	12	13	14
15	16	17	18	19	20	21
22	23	24	25	26	27	28
29	30	31				

November 2000

S	M	T	W	T	F	S
			1	2	3	4
5	6	7	8	9	10	11
12	13	14	15	16	17	18
19	20	21	22	23	24	25
26	27	28	29	30		

December 2000

S	M	T	W	T	F	S
					1	2
3	4	5	6	7	8	9
10	11	12	13	14	15	16
17	18	19	20	21	22	23
24	25	26	27	28	29	30
31						

Post Office Holidays

Dec 31, Jan 17, Feb 21, May 29, Jul 4,
Sep 4, Oct 9, Nov 10, Nov 23, Dec 25

Calendars

January 2001

S	M	T	W	T	F	S
	1	2	3	4	5	6
7	8	9	10	11	12	13
14	15	16	17	18	19	20
21	22	23	24	25	26	27
28	29	30	31			

February 2001

S	M	T	W	T	F	S
				1	2	3
4	5	6	7	8	9	10
11	12	13	14	15	16	17
18	19	20	21	22	23	24
25	26	27	28			

March 2001

S	M	T	W	T	F	S
				1	2	3
4	5	6	7	8	9	10
11	12	13	14	15	16	17
18	19	20	21	22	23	24
25	26	27	28	29	30	31

April 2001

S	M	T	W	T	F	S
1	2	3	4	5	6	7
8	9	10	11	12	13	14
15	16	17	18	19	20	21
22	23	24	25	26	27	28
29	30					

May 2001

S	M	T	W	T	F	S
		1	2	3	4	5
6	7	8	9	10	11	12
13	14	15	16	17	18	19
20	21	22	23	24	25	26
27	28	29	30	31		

June 2001

S	M	T	W	T	F	S
					1	2
3	4	5	6	7	8	9
10	11	12	13	14	15	16
17	18	19	20	21	22	23
24	25	26	27	28	29	30

July 2001

S	M	T	W	T	F	S
1	2	3	4	5	6	7
8	9	10	11	12	13	14
15	16	17	18	19	20	21
22	23	24	25	26	27	28
29	30	31				

August 2001

S	M	T	W	T	F	S
			1	2	3	4
5	6	7	8	9	10	11
12	13	14	15	16	17	18
19	20	21	22	23	24	25
26	27	28	29	30	31	

September 2001

S	M	T	W	T	F	S
						1
2	3	4	5	6	7	8
9	10	11	12	13	14	15
16	17	18	19	20	21	22
23	24	25	26	27	28	29
30						

October 2001

S	M	T	W	T	F	S
	1	2	3	4	5	6
7	8	9	10	11	12	13
14	15	16	17	18	19	20
21	22	23	24	25	26	27
28	29	30	31			

November 2001

S	M	T	W	T	F	S
				1	2	3
4	5	6	7	8	9	10
11	12	13	14	15	16	17
18	19	20	21	22	23	24
25	26	27	28	29	30	

December 2001

S	M	T	W	T	F	S
						1
2	3	4	5	6	7	8
9	10	11	12	13	14	15
16	17	18	19	20	21	22
23	24	25	26	27	28	29
30	31					

Post Office Holidays

Jan 1, Jan 15, Feb 19, May 28, Jul 4,
Sep 3, Oct 8, Nov 12, Nov 22, Dec 25

Calendars

January 2002

S	M	T	W	T	F	S
		1	2	3	4	5
6	7	8	9	10	11	12
13	14	15	16	17	18	19
20	21	22	23	24	25	26
27	28	29	30	31		

February 2002

S	M	T	W	T	F	S
					1	2
3	4	5	6	7	8	9
10	11	12	13	14	15	16
17	18	19	20	21	22	23
24	25	26	27	28		

March 2002

S	M	T	W	T	F	S
					1	2
3	4	5	6	7	8	9
10	11	12	13	14	15	16
17	18	19	20	21	22	23
24	25	26	27	28	29	30
31						

April 2002

S	M	T	W	T	F	S
	1	2	3	4	5	6
7	8	9	10	11	12	13
14	15	16	17	18	19	20
21	22	23	24	25	26	27
28	29	30				

May 2002

S	M	T	W	T	F	S
			1	2	3	4
5	6	7	8	9	10	11
12	13	14	15	16	17	18
19	20	21	22	23	24	25
26	27	28	29	30	31	

June 2002

S	M	T	W	T	F	S
						1
2	3	4	5	6	7	8
9	10	11	12	13	14	15
16	17	18	19	20	21	22
23	24	25	26	27	28	29
30						

July 2002

S	M	T	W	T	F	S
	1	2	3	4	5	6
7	8	9	10	11	12	13
14	15	16	17	18	19	20
21	22	23	24	25	26	27
28	29	30	31			

August 2002

S	M	T	W	T	F	S
				1	2	3
4	5	6	7	8	9	10
11	12	13	14	15	16	17
18	19	20	21	22	23	24
25	26	27	28	29	30	31

September 2002

S	M	T	W	T	F	S
1	2	3	4	5	6	7
8	9	10	11	12	13	14
15	16	17	18	19	20	21
22	23	24	25	26	27	28
29	30					

October 2002

S	M	T	W	T	F	S
		1	2	3	4	5
6	7	8	9	10	11	12
13	14	15	16	17	18	19
20	21	22	23	24	25	26
27	28	29	30	31		

November 2002

S	M	T	W	T	F	S
					1	2
3	4	5	6	7	8	9
10	11	12	13	14	15	16
17	18	19	20	21	22	23
24	25	26	27	28	29	30

December 2002

S	M	T	W	T	F	S
1	2	3	4	5	6	7
8	9	10	11	12	13	14
15	16	17	18	19	20	21
22	23	24	25	26	27	28
29	30	31				

Post Office Holidays

Jan 1, Jan 21, Feb 18, May 27, Jul 4,
Sep 2, Oct 14, Nov 11, Nov 28, Dec 25

Calendars

January 2003

S	M	T	W	T	F	S
			1	2	3	4
5	6	7	8	9	10	11
12	13	14	15	16	17	18
19	20	21	22	23	24	25
26	27	28	29	30	31	

February 2003

S	M	T	W	T	F	S
						1
2	3	4	5	6	7	8
9	10	11	12	13	14	15
16	17	18	19	20	21	22
23	24	25	26	27	28	

March 2003

S	M	T	W	T	F	S
						1
2	3	4	5	6	7	8
9	10	11	12	13	14	15
16	17	18	19	20	21	22
23	24	25	26	27	28	29
30	31					

April 2003

S	M	T	W	T	F	S
		1	2	3	4	5
6	7	8	9	10	11	12
13	14	15	16	17	18	19
20	21	22	23	24	25	26
27	28	29	30			

May 2003

S	M	T	W	T	F	S
				1	2	3
4	5	6	7	8	9	10
11	12	13	14	15	16	17
18	19	20	21	22	23	24
25	26	27	28	29	30	31

June 2003

S	M	T	W	T	F	S
1	2	3	4	5	6	7
8	9	10	11	12	13	14
15	16	17	18	19	20	21
22	23	24	25	26	27	28
29	30					

July 2003

S	M	T	W	T	F	S
		1	2	3	4	5
6	7	8	9	10	11	12
13	14	15	16	17	18	19
20	21	22	23	24	25	26
27	28	29	30	31		

August 2003

S	M	T	W	T	F	S
					1	2
3	4	5	6	7	8	9
10	11	12	13	14	15	16
17	18	19	20	21	22	23
24	25	26	27	28	29	30
31						

September 2003

S	M	T	W	T	F	S
	1	2	3	4	5	6
7	8	9	10	11	12	13
14	15	16	17	18	19	20
21	22	23	24	25	26	27
28	29	30				

October 2003

S	M	T	W	T	F	S
			1	2	3	4
5	6	7	8	9	10	11
12	13	14	15	16	17	18
19	20	21	22	23	24	25
26	27	28	29	30	31	

November 2003

S	M	T	W	T	F	S
						1
2	3	4	5	6	7	8
9	10	11	12	13	14	15
16	17	18	19	20	21	22
23	24	25	26	27	28	29
30						

December 2003

S	M	T	W	T	F	S
	1	2	3	4	5	6
7	8	9	10	11	12	13
14	15	16	17	18	19	20
21	22	23	24	25	26	27
28	29	30	31			

Post Office Holidays

Jan 1, Jan 20, Feb 17, May 26, Jul 4,
Sep 1, Oct 13, Nov 11, Nov 27, Dec 25

Calendars

January 2004

S	M	T	W	T	F	S
				1	2	3
4	5	6	7	8	9	10
11	12	13	14	15	16	17
18	19	20	21	22	23	24
25	26	27	28	29	30	31

February 2004

S	M	T	W	T	F	S
1	2	3	4	5	6	7
8	9	10	11	12	13	14
15	16	17	18	19	20	21
22	23	24	25	26	27	28
29						

March 2004

S	M	T	W	T	F	S
	1	2	3	4	5	6
7	8	9	10	11	12	13
14	15	16	17	18	19	20
21	22	23	24	25	26	27
28	29	30	31			

April 2004

S	M	T	W	T	F	S
				1	2	3
4	5	6	7	8	9	10
11	12	13	14	15	16	17
18	19	20	21	22	23	24
25	26	27	28	29	30	

May 2004

S	M	T	W	T	F	S
						1
2	3	4	5	6	7	8
9	10	11	12	13	14	15
16	17	18	19	20	21	22
23	24	25	26	27	28	29
30	31					

June 2004

S	M	T	W	T	F	S
		1	2	3	4	5
6	7	8	9	10	11	12
13	14	15	16	17	18	19
20	21	22	23	24	25	26
27	28	29	30			

July 2004

S	M	T	W	T	F	S
				1	2	3
4	5	6	7	8	9	10
11	12	13	14	15	16	17
18	19	20	21	22	23	24
25	26	27	28	29	30	31

August 2004

S	M	T	W	T	F	S
1	2	3	4	5	6	7
8	9	10	11	12	13	14
15	16	17	18	19	20	21
22	23	24	25	26	27	28
29	30	31				

September 2004

S	M	T	W	T	F	S
			1	2	3	4
5	6	7	8	9	10	11
12	13	14	15	16	17	18
19	20	21	22	23	24	25
26	27	28	29	30		

October 2004

S	M	T	W	T	F	S
					1	2
3	4	5	6	7	8	9
10	11	12	13	14	15	16
17	18	19	20	21	22	23
24	25	26	27	28	29	30
31						

November 2004

S	M	T	W	T	F	S
	1	2	3	4	5	6
7	8	9	10	11	12	13
14	15	16	17	18	19	20
21	22	23	24	25	26	27
28	29	30				

December 2004

S	M	T	W	T	F	S
			1	2	3	4
5	6	7	8	9	10	11
12	13	14	15	16	17	18
19	20	21	22	23	24	25
26	27	28	29	30	31	

Post Office Holidays

Jan 1, Jan 19, Feb 16, May 31, Jul 5,
Sep 6, Oct 11, Nov 11, Nov 25, Dec 24

To-Do List

To-Do List

To-Do List

To-Do List

To-Do List

Addresses and Phone Numbers

Name:
Address:
City, State, Zip:
Phone Number:

Name:
Address:
City, State, Zip:
Phone Number:

Name:
Address:
City, State, Zip:
Phone Number:

Name:
Address:
City, State, Zip:
Phone Number:

Name:
Address:
City, State, Zip:
Phone Number:

Name:
Address:
City, State, Zip:
Phone Number:

Name:
Address:
City, State, Zip:
Phone Number:

Addresses and Phone Numbers

Name:
Address:
City, State, Zip:
Phone Number:

Name:
Address:
City, State, Zip:
Phone Number:

Name:
Address:
City, State, Zip:
Phone Number:

Name:
Address:
City, State, Zip:
Phone Number:

Name:
Address:
City, State, Zip:
Phone Number:

Name:
Address:
City, State, Zip:
Phone Number:

Name:
Address:
City, State, Zip:
Phone Number:

Addresses and Phone Numbers

Name:
Address:
City, State, Zip:
Phone Number:

Name:
Address:
City, State, Zip:
Phone Number:

Name:
Address:
City, State, Zip:
Phone Number:

Name:
Address:
City, State, Zip:
Phone Number:

Name:
Address:
City, State, Zip:
Phone Number:

Name:
Address:
City, State, Zip:
Phone Number:

Name:
Address:
City, State, Zip:
Phone Number:

Addresses and Phone Numbers

Name:
Address:
City, State, Zip:
Phone Number:

Name:
Address:
City, State, Zip:
Phone Number:

Name:
Address:
City, State, Zip:
Phone Number:

Name:
Address:
City, State, Zip:
Phone Number:

Name:
Address:
City, State, Zip:
Phone Number:

Name:
Address:
City, State, Zip:
Phone Number:

Name:
Address:
City, State, Zip:
Phone Number:

Comments

Please fill and send the following to PCTA. Thank you!

a) Content

Is there any information you would want to have added as a new section?

Are there any changes to the trail?

Is there any section you would want removed?

b) Design

Are the sections ordered to allow quick access?

Comments

Is the presentation of the trail information comfortable to use?

Are the Water Alerts too close, too far, just right?

c) Use

Any other use not listed in the preface?

The Pacific Crest Trail Association
A Voice for the Trail

The Pacific Crest Trail Association is an effective advocate for the protection and wise management of this unique resource. Through our bi-monthly newsletter, publications, toll-free telephone number and Internet Web page, the association reports route changes, pending legislation, trail conditions and activities, which might threaten the largely pristine trail corridor.

Without constant attention, the trail would quickly succumb to the effects of humans and the forces of nature. Working in partnership with the US Forest Service, the National Park Service, the Bureau of Land Management, as well as state and private landowners, the Association organizes volunteer crews to help preserve the trail. Members also gather and report trail conditions which are relayed to appropriate officials.

The Association encourages good trail ethics, no trace camping and an awareness of the Pacific Crest National Scenic Trail as a valued national heritage.

The mission of the Pacific Crest Trail Association is to protect, preserve and promote the Pacific Crest National Scenic Trail so as to reflect its world-class significance for the enjoyment, education and adventure of hikers and equestrians.

The PCTA is a 501(c)(3) tax-exempt nonprofit organization. Your membership and donations are our number one way to keep this national treasure alive... Join us!

Pacific Crest Trail Association
Membership Benefits

- Six issues of the *PCT Communicator*
- A PCTA membership card
- Wilderness permits for travel in excess of 500 miles on the PCT
- 10% discount on PCT Store items (guidebooks, t-shirts, patches, etc.)
- 10% discount on PCTA activities (Campfest, Annual Meeting, etc.)
- A PCT decal
- Free trip partner listings in the PCT Communicator
- Free completion certificate for completing the trail
- The knowledge that your membership helps to protect and preserve the PCT for future generations

Yes! I want to join the PCTA team that preserves and protects the Pacific Crest Trail. Enclosed is my annual contribution of:

_____$35 Individual
_____$45 Family
_____$20 Limited Income
_____$75 Trail Partner
_____$75 Nonprofit Partner
_____$100 Sustainer
_____$500 Trail Builder
_____$1,000Lifetime

Name____

Address____

City_________________________State_____Zip_______________

I'd like to help out with trail projects, please call me at (   )__________

Payment by: Check MasterCard Visa

____
Cardholder Signature

____
Card Number Expiration Date

Mail to: Pacific Crest Trail Association, 5325 Elkhorn Blvd PMB 256, Sacramento, CA 95842

ぼくの 最愛の もの、
これが 全部 夢 ならば、
ああ、目覚めたくはなし。

My Beloved,
If this is all a dream,
Then, I do not want to wake up.